Clutter
Busters

Winning the battle against Clutter, Chaos, and Disorder Through Organization

BOOT CAMP FOR HOMEMAKERS

Clutter Busters

by Pat Calkins

ISBN-13: 978-0-9741366-2-2
ISBN-10: 0-9741366-2-X

Library of Congress Control Number: Available upon request

Book design by Kathryn E. Campbell

Book printing by Gorham Printing, Rochester, WA USA

CONTENTS

Chapter 1   **Welcome to Boot Camp** / **13**

Chapter 2   **Getting Organized (The right way!)** / **21**

Chapter 3   **Ready, Set, "Go Fish"** / **25**

Chapter 4   **"Three-Step/Jump Start"** / **33**

Chapter 5   **"ASAP"** / **45**

Chapter 6   **"Taking Responsibility"** / **55**

Chapter 7   **To Train, or Not to Train? What a Silly Question** / **65**

Chapter 8   **Drill Sergeant "Mom"** / **69**

Chapter 9   **The Dime Game** / **73**

Chapter 10   **Work Smarter—not Harder** / **85**

Chapter 11   **The Five-Step Snappy Daily Routine** / **91**

Chapter 12   **Step #1 of Your Snappy Daily Routine** / **97**

Chapter 13   **Step #2 of Your Snappy Daily Routine** / **107**

Chapter 14   **Step #3 of Your Snappy Daily Routine** / **111**

Chapter 15   **Step #4 of Your Snappy Daily Routine** / **117**

Chapter 16   **Step #5 of Your Snappy Daily Routine** / **121**

Chapter 17   **When You're Done, You're Done!** / **133**

Chapter 18   **Lights Out!** / **135**

Chapter 19   **Graduation Day Kudos to You, Soldier** / **137**

Just a Little
"FYI"

Although this book is addressed to "women" (wives, mothers and homemakers), it is not exclusively for this gender or those holding these titles.

There are men I know who have, either by choice or out of necessity, assumed the role of caretaker of the home and primary caregiver to the children. To these exceptional gentlemen, I say, BRAVO! My hat's off to you. In my opinion, you have taken on the toughest job known to mankind (or womankind). Therefore, let it be known that any and all references to the "wife or mother " throughout this book can be interchanged to say the "husband or father" as well.

By the same token, many single men and women live on their own in a house, apartment, or a dorm room in college. For this segment of our society, the need for order in their lives is just as important as it is for anyone else.

And while I am at it, I may as well go on to say that children living at home can also benefit greatly from learning the principles in this book. If you learn them now, you can save yourself a lot of Tylenol headaches later in life.

Let's face it, clutter is nondiscriminatory! It is not reserved for women only, for parents exclusively, for married people, or for someone of a certain age. No indeed! It can strike anyone, anywhere, anytime. So absolutely no one should feel left out while reading this book. It is for everyone who has ever had a desire to gain control of their lives!

May the tips, hints, and practical helps in this book set you on your road to success. Whether you are a complete neat-freak, totally disorganized, or anything in between, you will gain insight from the humorous stories, embarrassing incidents, and transparent confessions found in this book. If you are even slightly domestically-challenged, take heart. There is help for you. And you can also take comfort in knowing that you are not alone. Millions suffer from this disorder.

Who knows, someday there may be a pill to solve this problem, but until then, we just have to take care of it the old-fashioned way… fighting the battle head-on! You can do it. I know you can.

Let me assure you of one thing, I am passionately dedicated to your success!

INTRODUCTION

*T*here should be a law against it, you know, but there's not. We do it every day. We send poor, unsuspecting brides blissfully strolling into marriage without the training they need to succeed. (Or, in some cases, just to survive.) Shame on us! What must we be we thinking?

That would never happen in the corporate world…

Imagine for a moment that you have just been hired by a big corporation to fill a very important position—not an entry-level position—but as manager of the entire company! You are now the leader, the director, the one in charge, the one who is responsible to make sure everything runs smoothly. You and you alone are the one everyone else looks to for leadership and guidance. Your company lives or dies by the decisions you make.

Now imagine (gulp!) that you were never trained for this position. You have no experience and no idea how to do the job. How long do you think your company would survive with you in charge?

Well, what about in your home? Did you ever consider the fact that when you got married, know it or not—like it or not, you signed on as manager? It's true. And with that job comes a whole lot of responsibility and pressure.

Now, add to that pressure, the fact that today more moms work outside the home than ever before. And still, in most cases, the care of the home falls squarely on her shoulders.

As wife, mother, and homemaker you are expected to assume the role of manager of your home. You are the one in charge of making the decisions that effect how efficiently your home operates, how neat and tidy it looks, how warm and inviting it feels, how economically it runs, and how peaceful and loving it's atmosphere is. But how well were you trained for this position of extreme leadership? In school, were you taught the skills you need for this important position? How about at home when you were growing up; did your mom take you under her wing and train you diligently? Or, were you just thrust into the job with a "good luck, kid, hope you make it" attitude?

Unfortunately, the latter is what happened to many (if not most) of us. Apparently, it was just assumed that we would magically know how to manage our homes because we had reached the legal age of adulthood or because we had somehow managed to convince our wobbly legs to carry us down that long aisle of the church where Prince Charming was waiting. Either of these two events must have meant we were automatically ready, right?

Wrong!

When the dust settled from all the hoop-la of the wedding ceremony and the glow of the honeymoon wore off, we suddenly faced a new and startling reality: EEE, GADS! WE ARE IN CHARGE! For many of us, it was a frightening realization!

There should have been a transitional step (preferably mandatory) between the home we grew up in and the home we were suddenly put in charge of.

With the advent of a barrage of reality shows on TV, I can imagine a new one called: *Boot Camp for Homemakers*. It would include a tough and demanding training regimen designed to prepare the future homemaker for whatever a home, husband, and a few children could throw her way. I can imagine, after a while, the strain becoming too much for some of the recruits and them breaking down. The stress clearly showing on their faces, and with a child wrapped around each leg, they look directly into the camera lens and cry, "I can't take it any more. Get me out of here."

I know the feeling. I uttered those exact words many times when my children were small and I found myself suddenly thrust into "on the job, learn-as-you-go" training.

It's Sink or Swim, Baby!

I don't think that pushing someone into the deep end of a swimming pool is a very good way to teach them to swim. Now, I'm no lifeguard, but it seems to me that drowning is a very real possibility. Likewise, when we send poor, unsuspecting brides into marriage without proper training, I'm afraid that drowning for them is also a very real possibility.

Positions of extreme leadership require extreme training. And Managing a Home is one of the most extreme jobs on all the earth. There is so much at stake. The fabric of our society is made up of homes and families at its very core. As goes the home, so goes the nation. This extremely important job should never be taken lightly! We need to educate and equip every homemaker as though the well being of our nation depends on it. Because, you know what?...it does. We *MUST* stop pushing them into the pool without first teaching them to swim.

I walked into marriage a blissful young bride with no clue what I was getting myself into, and trial-and-error (with the emphasis on *error*) was the only education system available to me at the time.

But things are different today. It is time we stand up and tell the fledgling bride, "Don't do it. Don't go into marriage unprepared. You don't have to any more! There's help available." Hog-tie her if necessary, but don't let her do it.

And if YOU are that bride-to-be, don't let YOURSELF go into marriage unprepared.

But, what if you are already married and you're struggling to keep your head above water? Is it too late? NO! It's not! It's never too late. It wasn't for me, and it certainly isn't for you.

Hang on! Help is on the way!

Clutter Busters will help train and equip you to successfully fulfill your role of extreme leadership.

CHAPTER 1

Welcome to Boot Camp

*O*nce upon a time, long, long ago, I was a struggling young wife, mother, and homemaker. My days were hectic. My house was a wreck. My nerves were shattered and I was up to my eyeballs in clutter, chaos and disorder. My life was such a mess that there were times when I had the distinct feeling I was at the end of my rope. Help!!!! It wasn't supposed to be this way…

> *As a little girl growing up, I often daydreamed about what kind of a wife and mother I would someday become. Of course, in that dream-like state, I always saw myself as one of the great super heroes of homemakers. I was Wonder Wife, Super Mom and Homemaker Extraordinaire all rolled into one. I frequently pictured myself standing on top of the world with my hands on my hips. In this scene I was wearing a bright blue shirt with a large red "S" (S-for Super Mom) plastered right in the middle of the chest. I had on red tights and a blue cape that billowed softly in the breeze behind me. And, as the crowning touch, there was a golden halo floating delicately above my head.*
>
> *In this dream, my house was a show place. It was so clean that you almost needed sunglasses to protect your eyes from the shine. My children were perfect little angels with*

crisp clean clothes, perfectly combed hair and impeccable manners. My husband, of course, was none other than Prince Charming himself who had whisked me away on his white horse to live with him in his castle on a hill.

Yes, indeed, if there was a Pulitzer Prize for Homemaking, I was going to win it!

You see, I had it all planned out. So that by the time my Prince Charming (Tom) really did come along and carry me away with him, I was ready to start living the dream I had had all my life. Although I was quite young, as brides go, I was absolutely confident about my ability to make my dream come true. And, even though I *had* spent a lot of time daydreaming as a little girl, my confidence was not simply based upon idle wishes and pie-in-the-sky dreams. No, sirree! It was based on concrete evidence. I had three distinct benefits going for me—three valid reasons for being so confident.

Reason #1 Growing up, I had been diligently taught by my mother every imaginable aspect of cleaning a house. I could do everything from cleaning a toilet until it shined to making a bed with perfect hospital corners and covers so tight you could bounce a quarter off them. I was proficient at dusting, vacuuming, sweeping and mopping. I could practically wash the dishes blindfolded and with one hand tied behind my back. At a very young age I could sort the laundry, operate the washer and dryer, and fold and put away the clean clothes. There was simply no chore I couldn't handle.

Reason #2 I had done a lot of babysitting in my teenage years. I had had so much experience changing diapers and feeding and burping and rocking babies that I almost felt like a mother long before I actually had a baby of my own.

Reason #3 But, by far, the most important benefit I had going for me was the level of desire I possessed. There was nothing in the world I wanted more than to be a great wife, mother, and homemaker. It was my one true passion in life. It was what I had dreamed of all my growing up years. While my peers dreamed of lofty careers with impressive titles and even more impressive paychecks, I dreamed only of making a great home for the family I would someday have.

From Daydream, to Nightmare

With all of these benefits going for me, I knew I couldn't help but be a raging success at my chosen career. There was just no way I could fail. And sure enough, for the entire duration of our honeymoon, I didn't. It was shortly thereafter, however, that I began to notice tell-tale signs of my halo beginning to slip... slowly at first, but gradually picking up steam.

Three years and two babies later, my halo was no where to be found. (It was probably buried under the piles of clutter somewhere.) My red tights had holes in the knees and my cape was dragging on the ground behind me. At the ripe old age of 21, I was washed up! A failure!

What happened? What went wrong?

I had entered into marriage with such high hopes. But now, on any given day, my house looked like it could qualify for federal disaster relief (and maybe even rushed to the head of the line).

Day in and day out, I worked hard trying to keep up with the demands of running a household and caring for my husband and two small children. But instead of getting better, things progressively got worse.

Oh, it wasn't as though our house *never* looked good. I *did* have my moments. Any time a situation called for it, such as, when company was coming for dinner or we were having friends over for some event, I could, by sheer will and grit, make our house look like it just hopped off the pages of *Better Homes and Gardens*. It wasn't easy, but it could be done. I had to start working weeks in advance, going from room to room cleaning, throwing-out, scrubbing, sweeping, shining and polishing. I worked from dawn until way beyond bedtime each day. But by party time, whoopee! I was ready. Our house was picture-perfect.

Of course, by the following day, I was so utterly exhausted that I needed complete bed-rest just to survive. Consequently, the all-to-predictable decline would begin immediately. And before I knew it, our house was right back to its usual bedraggled condition.

This was my life for years—up one day, down the next. (Well, it was actually more like up one day, down the next 20 or so.) It was so frustrating. I wanted off this roller coaster. I desperately wanted to succeed in the one area of my life where I really felt "called". It was a helpless feeling. But what made the situation even more bewildering was that I couldn't identify my problem. I was completely clueless as to what I was doing wrong. Honestly! I just did not know. I was beginning to suspect that I was either lazy or born to be a failure. Neither prospect was very flattering.

At least in all this misery, I was not alone. My dear friend and neighbor, Mary, was just as "out of control" as I was. We would often get together and lament about our situation. We would whine and complain until we were blue in our faces, but nothing ever changed. Neither of us had a clue as to how to take control of our lives.

Then one day Mary came to me with a newspaper article in her hand. She was trembling with excitement and almost breathless. It seemed there was a workshop being advertised in the paper that was due to start in just two weeks. It was a class on how to *get organized*. She was sure it was the answer to all our problems and said we should enroll right away. Ker-plop! She slapped the article down on my kitchen counter and eagerly awaited my response.

Now, wouldn't you think that a life ring, tossed right in the face of a drowning person, would be seized immediately? Especially, if that person was going down for the third time? Well, as remarkable as it sounds, it wasn't! I couldn't imagine that a class on organization would be able to teach me anything that my mother hadn't already taught me. So I politely told Mary that I wasn't interested in taking the class with her. I'll never forget the look on her face. It was one of shock and disbelief. She was so stunned that for almost a full minute she couldn't even speak. When she finally got her tongue back, she pleaded with me. She reasoned with me. She tried to knock some sense into my thick skull, but nothing she said or did affected me. I was standing stubbornly by my decision. So, with a sigh of exasperation, Mary picked up her life ring and went home.

For the next two weeks I tried to prove to Mary, to myself, and to the whole world that I didn't need any outside help. If I just put my mind to it, I could conquer my problem…on my own…thank you very much! (Sounds suspiciously like pride lifting its ugly head, don't you think?) So with all the determination and willpower I could muster, I worked like a horse to overcome the consequences of living like a pig. It soon became apparent, however, that I was fighting a losing battle and two days before the workshop was scheduled to begin, I came out waving a white flag.

"Mary," I blubbered into the phone. "I want to take that class with you."

Mary sounded thrilled with my decision, but mostly relieved because her friend had finally come to her senses.

So, two nights later, we attended the first session of the workshop on organization together. We came home from that class inspired and challenged. One night a week for the following four weeks we attended another session. Every week we learned new ideas and practical principles that *really worked* when we tried them at home. By the end of the workshop we were like two different women, forever transformed by the power of organization. We had gained a level of confidence and ability that neither of us had even imagined possible.

Although I will always be grateful to my mother for all of the homemaking skills she taught me, I discovered that there was something she did *not* teach me. And that is, *how to "manage" those skills.* You see, as long as my mother was there to tell me what to do and when to do it, my job was easy. All I had to do was obey her orders. But once I got married and my mother was no longer on the scene, I was like a ship lost at sea. It didn't seem to matter how many skills or abilities I had, I was at a loss as to how to take charge of my time, properly direct my efforts, and put those skills together in a workable order. Although I worked hard every day from sun up to sun set, I was like a hamster on an exercise wheel—generating lots of activity, but accomplishing very little.

But then one day all of that changed. A life ring was thrown to me while I was bobbing around helplessly in the water and I was rescued from almost certain destruction. That life ring was…*the power of organization at work in my life*! Now when I tackle chores, I get the absolute most done in the least amount of time—without sacrificing quality. No more spinning my wheels. No more wasting time.

Getting my life organized was revolutionizing! Organization affected every area of my life from my work, to my relationships, to my self-esteem. It freed me to pursue my dreams and empowered me to seize my destiny. I could sing its praises all day long. I don't know where I would be today with out the transforming power of organization at work in my life. I shudder to think!

When Destiny Comes Knocking At Your Door...
(What Will You Do?)

If you have been wanting to get your life in order, there is no better time than now to do it. Trust me, you will not regret your decision because "life is better" when you are organized. It is as plain and simple as that.

We all have a destiny to fulfill. But when destiny comes knocking at *your* door, what will you do? Will you answer the call boldly or will you run and hide under your bed?

Will you have to tell it to go away until another day because you have too many dishes to do, too much clutter to muddle through, and too little time to spend on anything except trying to dig yourself out from under the mess?

Who knows what you were born to do? Do you have a sense of your destiny? Whatever it is, don't you dare miss out because you are too overwhelmed by the clutter, chaos, and disorder in your life!

It is time to take back the control of your life, see your dreams fulfilled, and to lay hold of your destiny. And the power of organization will help you do just that!

There is almost no limit to the benefits that it will give you. If you want to:

- Stop your life from spinning out of control

- Be successful in pursuing your dreams

- Reduce your stress level

- Slash your workload

- Save money

- Have more time to do the things you *want* to do instead of the things you *have* to do

- Live life like a winner

- Improve your relationships (yes, even that!)

- And fulfill your destiny

Then, start by getting organized. It will make all the difference in the world. If this is what you truly want, then all I can say is…you go for it!

If you are jumping up and down right now shouting, "Yee Haw! I'm finally going to take control of my life. What a glorious day for me!" then let me be the first to congratulate you.

But let me also be the first to shake your hand and say, "Welcome aboard, soldier. You've just enlisted. So put on your camo, strap up your combat boots, and grab your weapon. Because, this isn't summer camp…it's BOOT CAMP! And what you will learn over the next few chapters will turn you into a well trained, confident, capable, lean, mean, clutter-fighting machine.

You will battle clutter, chaos and disorder and you WILL win! You will overcome the effects of loosey-goosey living through the incredible power of a disciplined life. You will be put through your paces, toughened and prepared.

You will get the training and experience you may have missed growing up. You will be exhausted at times, even mad at me at times, but that's OK, because it is all part of the boot camp experience. It is training to the extreme. It is preparation for your future, a future filled with hope and promise.

So, is everyone ready? "I CAN'T HEAR YOU!!!" Now, snap to attention, gals, and wipe that smile off your face. (Are you mad at me yet?) You are preparing for battle now and what you learn here at Boot Camp for Homemakers could save your life (or at least your sanity) and the lives (or sanity) of those around you. I won't be requiring you to shave your head but I definitely plan to shake up your life.

CHAPTER 2

Getting Organized
(The right way!)

*F*irst things first, not in reverse!

When you step off the bus into boot camp and your feet hit the dusty ground, the first thing you will have to do is change some of your old ways of thinking. For example, what comes to your mind when you hear the word *organization*? I know I used to have my own ideas about that. I thought that getting *organized* meant to get my things, my possessions, you know, my "stuff" in order.

To me, being organized meant having everything in my entire house perfectly arranged in neat little rows. I envisioned opening a closet door and seeing all the clothes hung precisely in place—shirts with shirts (starting with short sleeves and graduating up to long), pants with pants, and dresses with dresses. I imagined my kitchen cupboards meticulously organized right down to the spices in alphabetical order. I pictured my children's bedrooms flawlessly arranged and set up with easy to reach hooks for coats and hats and having lots of shelves for storing assorted toys in clear shoeboxes. I saw the medicine cabinets in our bathrooms with all the necessities placed on the shelves in meticulous order. I envisioned our linen closet with sheets and towels neatly folded and perfectly stacked.

This was my idea of organization. This was all I knew. Organization meant getting all my "stuff" in order. Nothing more, nothing less. And all of that IS good, but I have since learned that there is a great deal more to organization than just the "stuff". OH, BOY! Is there ever!

If you now believe as I once did, that organization is about getting all of your possessions in order, then your focus is in the wrong place. Organization is about more than just the "stuff". Of course, it includes the stuff, but it's just the tip of the iceberg. If you've never dealt with what's beneath that tip, then you've never given yourself the chance to truly succeed.

Organization starts on the INSIDE of you. Not the outside. First your life, then your stuff. It has to come in that order. Here's why I say that:

———

There are some new reality shows on TV these days that deal with the subject of organization. The premise of these shows is that some lucky family wins the right to be the featured guests of the week. These guests get to invite the whole world to take a close-up look at their grotesquely disorganized, frightfully messy home. The payoff for this humiliation is that a professional organizer swoops in and completely organizes one or more of the rooms of this family's house. The organizer begins by sorting and cleaning out absolutely everything in the targeted rooms.

On one of the programs, all of the "stuff" is taken out into the yard and put it into piles on huge tarps. Then they instruct the homeowners to sort through the piles (which, by the way, are usually enormous), putting things into three pre-set categories:

- To Keep

- To Toss

- To Sell

Once the sorting is done, only the things from the "to keep" pile are allowed to be taken back into the house. Then the professional organizer gets busy organizing everything the family chose to keep. The family is not allowed to watch this process as it takes place. I guess the reason for that is so they will be shocked and amazed when they step into the finished room and open their eyes. When everything is said and done, the results are usually quite impressive and the family really does look genuinely astonished. This transformation process takes place over a period of a several days but for the lucky TV viewer everything happens in just 30 minutes.

On another one of the programs, the homeowner is actually allowed to help in the organization process.

I enjoy watching these programs because I often pick up new and interesting ideas from them. And while I'm thrilled for the family whose home has been wondrously transformed by the pros, I can't help but wonder how long those amazing transformations will last. The problem is that the professionals didn't instill the family with the values or teach them the skills it takes to maintain their new found order. And if there is no change in lifestyle, then how can there be lasting results?

After all, you have to ask yourself the question, "*How* did that family get into such a mess in the first place?" What character trait did they possess that caused them to live that way? And, isn't that trait still alive and well? And if it is, then how on earth can they ever manage to *keep* everything organized?

I believe I know the answer to that question. *They can't!*

———

That is why I say that there is more to organization than merely getting your "stuff" in order. Back when I used to think that was what it was all about, had I gone through every closet, cupboard, and cabinet in my entire house and emptied them completely and organized every single item in them, what would those closets look like today? What would they have looked like six months down the road? I can tell you what. They would look like the *before* pictures of closets in the houses they feature on those TV reality shows. Because getting my "stuff"' organized would have just been treating the symptom of my problem rather than the cause. We've all heard the saying:

Give a man a fish, and you've fed him for a day.

— But —

Teach a man to fish and you've fed him for a lifetime.

The same is true of getting organized. You can hire a professional organizer to come into your home and work her buns off to get your whole house organized right down to your tiniest pair of earrings. She can put everything in its proper place and even adorn your home with cute little wicker baskets, clever pull out drawers with divided trays in them, and every Rubbermaid organizer ever manufactured, each filled with perfectly organized effects. Your whole house can look like the blue ribbon winner in a home organization contest when she is done, but what good will all of that do you in the long run? A few months from now, you will be calling her to come back and do it all over again because all she really did was to *give* you a fish. The only way to achieve lasting results is to go beyond the "stuff" and learn to *fish* for yourself.

How do you do that? You have to train yourself to have good habits in your life! You have to adopt the values that will shape your future. And you have to learn the skills that it takes to successfully manage your home, your life, and your family. Only then can you become a truly organized person. Because organization is not just an activity that you perform once and forget it—it is a WAY OF LIFE!

Consequently, much of what you will be reading about in this book goes beyond the "stuff" so that you can learn to *fish* for yourself and become a truly organized person—not just a person with *temporarily* organized stuff.

Treat the cause, not the symptom!

CHAPTER 3

Ready, Set, "Go Fish"

Since the time that Mary and I took that workshop on organization, I have had a burning desire to learn more. That class whetted my appetite to the point that I began to gobble up every bit of information I could lay my hands on. There was, of course, no literal, physical Boot Camp for Homemakers that I could attend, so I had to do scads of research to come up with the information I craved. I read countless books and magazine articles on the subject, attended several other classes and seminars, and interviewed scores of women whom I considered to be at least *somewhat* organized. All in an attempt to learn everything I could. I had experienced first-hand the benefits that being organized could give, and I didn't want to miss a single speck. I absolutely *loved* the whole concept.

But I will have to admit that my first-ever introduction into the world of organization was a strange experience for me. It all began with the workshop that Mary and I took together…

> *We were both hopelessly disorganized and it seemed as if this class might be our last hope. We were eager to learn anything we could to help us get our lives straightened out.*
>
> *The workshop was being held in the evenings at a local church in our area. We arrived at the church for the first of*

five classes that made up the workshop and we found the room where the class was being held. We chose a table and sat down. We were a little nervous, a little apprehensive, but mostly excited.

We had to wait through what seemed like an endless stream of introductions and preliminaries before the class actually began. But finally, at long last, our instructor opened her book and began to speak. I poised my pen over my notepad and breathlessly waited to hear the principles of organization that were going to set me free and change my life forever. But when our instructor began to speak, the things she said didn't seem to have anything to do with getting organized whatsoever. In fact, I glanced around the room to make sure that we hadn't accidentally stumbled into the wrong classroom.

As it turned out, we were in the right room, all right. It's just that I was so ignorant concerning the basic principles of organization that I wouldn't have recognized them if they had jumped up and bitten me on my nose. Of course, I later learned that these principles really did apply and that they work amazingly well. I discovered that there is a great deal more to organization than neatly stacking your bathroom towels or arranging your kitchen in a logical order.

I shared this little story for a reason. Some of the principles you will read about in this book may strike you the same way. You may turn your book over and look at the cover to make sure that it is actually a book dealing with organization. Let me assure you that these principles really *do* apply to organization. In fact, I would go so far as to say that you can't be truly organized without first having these principles firmly established in your life. Anyone who tells you differently is only interested in "giving you a fish".

But I want you to learn "how to fish"! So get out your hooks, grab onto a wiggly worm, and get ready to cast your line, girls. We're goin' fishin'!

Where To Start

First of all, if you are going fishing, you have to have the right equipment. And what you need can't be purchased at your local sporting goods store. In fact, it can't be purchased at all. Nope! You can't buy it anywhere. You can't order it on line or from a catalog, or find it at a department store. If you could, it would be worth a fortune. No, unfortunately, this particular piece of equipment has to be homemade by "you". You can't even bribe someone else into making it for you. You and you alone must make it. It takes hard work, practice, consistency and determination, but once you have it fully formed and fashioned and operating at peak efficiency, it will be one of your most treasured possessions. It will serve you well all the days of your life.

What Is It?

It's one of those necessary requirements for becoming organized. It isn't terribly glamorous. In fact, it is often referred to as the dreaded "D" word. At first, you may think this requirement couldn't possibly have anything to do with organization. But to tell the truth, the "D" word is foundational to organization, whether we like it or not.

And just what is that dreaded *"D"* word? It's "Discipline"! (You knew that was coming, didn't you?) Ouch! We don't like that word. We don't want to feel controlled, the way we were when we were children. We want to be free. After all, we are adults now and we should be able to do what we want, when we want, and without anyone or anything controlling us and telling us what we can or cannot do. That's what freedom is all about, right?

Well, I must confess, that that is exactly the way I used to feel. After I got married and was no longer under the rule of my parents, and especially the rule of my mother who required me to do certain household chores at certain times, I felt as though I had been set free. I was an adult now who could just do whatever her little ol' heart desired. There were no expectations, no guidelines, and no rules. Yippee! I was free!

Oddly enough, however, this freedom bore a striking resemblance to a stone-cold prison…complete with bars and chains. I was not in control of my life or my circumstances; they were in control of me. And they did a pretty good job of keeping me locked up in a prison of guilt and shame, not to mention frustration, anxiety and depression.

Then one day, I began to experience *real* freedom. And can you guess where it came from? That's right…from *discipline.*

You see, once my mom wasn't there to direct my every move I had thought that life was going to be a walk in the park, a picnic, a non-stop party. I was in the enviable position of being able to determine for myself when *I* wanted to do things, like say, the dishes, for example. And since the decision was mine to make, I usually didn't bother do them right after a meal. Why? Because…I didn't have to! Sometimes I didn't do them after two meals. And sometimes, I didn't do them for days at a time. It felt pretty good, at first, being my own boss. But guess what, those dishes *always* came back to haunt me. And one day, as I was standing at the kitchen sink doing several days worth of dirty dishes, I realized that being the one in control wasn't as much fun as I thought it was going to be.

Well, duuuh! I wonder if that's because I wasn't really the one in control after all. *My circumstances were!*

But then along came discipline, that rigid, bossy, domineering, nagging little voice of authority that I had always thought was so villainous. And now all of a sudden, it became the hero instead of the villain. The reason is simple. Because of what it did for my life. It helped me take control of my circumstances, and literally gave me the *freedom* to enjoy my life, my home, and my family. And it can do the same for you.

Where Does This Discipline Come From?

This discipline doesn't come from your mother. It doesn't come from your husband. It doesn't come from your best friend. It can come from only one person… you! That nagging little voice of authority is your own. Because the discipline I'm talking about is "self" discipline. I sometimes think it would be a whole lot *easier* for us if there *was* another person standing over us giving orders and shaking a big stick in our face. That way we would have no choice but to comply. But when the voice of authority is our own, it isn't always so easy to listen and obey. And why is that? Because there are no consequences when we don't obey—or, so we think! In reality however, there really *are* consequences. Big ones. Painful ones. Consequences that cost us our freedom, peace, and joy. And these are much more damaging to us than the ones we might get from someone wielding a big stick.

I think we often see our miserable circumstances (the clutter, the mess, the confusion, the frustration, the discord, the stress) and we don't even recognize them for what they really are…the consequences of our own lack of self-discipline. Instead we somehow see ourselves as poor, unfortunate victims who didn't have a choice in the whole matter. Poor us!

Well, guess what, girls. It's time to wake up and smell the latte'! You and you alone are responsible for your circumstances. No one else. And that also means that you and you alone have to take the responsibility to "fix it". And the only way you can do that is through discipline, you know, that dreaded "D" word.

But cheer up! It's not that bad. At first I, too, bristled at the whole idea of discipline, then, gradually, I began to accept it, and now I love it. I love it because of what it does for my life. But it didn't come naturally for me. I often had to take myself by the nap of the neck and literally force myself to do the things I knew I should, *when* I should. Sometimes I went along kicking and screaming because I didn't *want to* do them then or didn't *feel like* it at the time. But it was during those times, when I forced myself to be good and do the things I knew I should even though I really, really, really didn't feel like it, that I benefited the very most. Because when I did them despite the way I *felt*, I noticed a strength building inside me, much the same way that physical exercise builds strength in our bodies.

The Amazing Transformation

There is a beautiful thing about self-discipline. I know that, at first, it is no fun (I've had more fun going to the dentist). But after a while it begins to quietly take on a whole different nature—kind of like a caterpillar that becomes a butterfly.

The wonderful, magical thing that happens to discipline is that it slowly turns from a drudgery into a…habit.

A habit, according to Mr. Webster (loosely translated), is something that is done so often it becomes automatic and therefore is hard to break. It is a tendency to perform a certain action or behave in a certain way until it becomes the usual way of doing things. In other words, it becomes…the norm.

The Great Exchange

We all have habits, some good and some bad. Obviously we would like to break the bad ones and keep the good ones. But it isn't always easy to break the bad ones (just ask anyone who has ever smoked). Back in the early days of our marriage, my life was just full of bad habits (thankfully, smoking was not one of them). But I had so many poor "*work*" habits that my life was spinning out of control. But, once I started regaining control, I discovered that the best way to break a bad habit was to replace it with a good one. And that, my dear friends, is accomplished with discipline. It is the great exchange.

The 21 Day Challenge

How do we exchange a bad habit for a good one? With self-discipline, repetition, and consistency. But most of all with 21 consecutive days. Here's how it works. In the next few chapters I will be sharing with you "three" of the most important habits you will ever need in order to be truly organized—AND—to stay that way.

These habits are not earth shattering. They're not rocket science. In fact, they are ridiculously simple. And yet, for all their simplicity, so many of us have completely missed them. So, if you are one of the thousands of women who has never developed these good habits, may I encourage you to take "21 Day Challenge" so that you can get them established in your life. It may not be easy. In fact, I can guarantee that it won't be. But let me assure you that if you develop these 3 GREAT habits in your life, the rewards will be so incredibly worth while that you will *forever* be grateful that you did.

The 21-day challenge goes like this: Whatever habit you wish to develop in your life MUST be practiced, without fail, for twenty-one consecutive days. And that means…faithfully, never missing a single day.

The idea behind this, according to the experts, is that any action consistently repeated for 21 *consecutive* days becomes a habit. That means that if, on day 10, you skip doing it, you must start over with day number one. It has to be 21 *consecutive* days. And then, after another 10 days, a habit becomes a way of life (either good or bad).

As you begin to develop these habits, they may, at first, feel like sheer drudgery. It may take all the inner strength you can muster to do them faithfully. You may even find yourself copping a bit of an attitude around day 10 or 15, because you simply don't want to do them any more. But take heart! Be strong! Hang in there! And what ever you do, don't quit!!!

And then, on that grand and glorious 21st morning, you will wake up and notice that there is something different about you. Something has changed. The caterpillar has become a butterfly. You will find yourself doing these things without even thinking about them. They will be so natural that you will feel as though you've done them this way all of your life (and the best part of all is—you wouldn't go back to your old way of doing things for anything). What happened to you? The 21 days that you spent diligently training yourself was your cocoon time. Through self-discipline, you stayed in that cocoon until your transformation was complete. And once you emerged, you found that you had replaced those old, sloppy habits, for brand new, extraordinary, life-giving ones. And you are one step closer to realizing your dream of being organized because of it.

A Fish Story

No one walked through your front door and handed you a free, unearned fish that will be here today and gone tomorrow. No, indeed! You earned this one, baby! You worked, you toiled, you threaded that worm onto the hook, you cast your line, you waited patiently, and you reeled in that fish all on your own. Do you realize what's happening? You are learning the principles and developing the habits that will "feed" you for a lifetime. WAY TO GO!

CHAPTER 4

Great Habit #1

"Three-Step/Jump Start"

$\mathcal{U}$p to this point, you have been in Boot Camp Orientation. Now it is time to actually begin your training. There may be dozens of good habits that you will develop over time as you work toward your goal of becoming organized. But there are three habits that go way beyond good, all the way to *great!*

The first one is called the Three-Step/Jump-Start Habit.

Imagine, if you will, the sound of a trumpet blaring at the crack of dawn. This is reveille, the call to, "wake-up, sleepy head, and get out of bed". It is not a suggestion. It is a command. The military does not allow anyone the luxury of ignoring the message conveyed by this peppy little tune. In the military, they mean business, and so do I. (Remember…it is not my job to make you like me, rather to make you successful.)

If you want to develop the habits in your life that will set you free and help you reach the goals you have set for yourself, then consider the fact that you will most likely have to overcome some sloppy habits in your life. And what's the best way to do that? By replacing them with good ones, right?

The first good habit just happens to be three mini-habits all rolled into one. It is called the Three-Step/Jump-Start and it will give you a literal "jump start" on your day. It will get the ball rolling in the right direction as soon as your feet hit the floor in the morning. With the Three-Step/Jump-Start, there is no turning back.

Dead Battery

If you've ever been stranded because your car had a dead battery, then you how know frustrating and inconvenient it can be. You also know just how valuable a jump-start can be in this situation. Some thoughtful person comes along in your hour of need and fastens one end of a pair of jumper cables to the terminals of your dead battery and the other end to the terminals of a live battery. Thus the juice from the live battery transfers over to your dead battery, giving it the "spark" it needs to get your car going.

That is the idea behind the Three-Step/Jump-Start. Sometimes when you get up in the morning, you may feel like your "battery" is dead. There is so much work to do that you hardly know where to start, and to be frank, not starting at all sounds pretty tempting. So you throw on your bathrobe, cinch up the belt, grab a piece of toast and a glass of milk, and plop down in front of the TV for a few minutes of reality escape (which sometimes turns into a few hours).

This kind of "failure" mentality is not allowed here at Boot Camp! You are a winner. You have a destiny to fulfill. Now act like it!

Discipline yourself to follow the three simple steps of the Three-Step/Jump-Start every morning. When you do you will be giving your "battery" the spark it needs to get you going. And once you get going, accomplishments will begin to pile up. And these accomplishments will feed something very important inside you—your self-confidence.

"Self-confidence"— A Powerful Role In Your Success

When there is a lack of self-confidence you can end up feeling "defeated before you ever begin". Has a quick glance around your house ever made you feel so overwhelmed that all you wanted to do was crawl back into your unmade bed and pull the covers over your head? Have you ever thought, "Why do I even bother trying?"

When these types of feelings weigh you down, you see yourself as a failure. And before you know it, you begin to act like one. By contrast, however, when you see yourself as a winner, you begin to feel and act like a winner.

This is an all-important self-evaluation. Why is it so important? Because it determines the degree of success you will experience in life. *Confidence breeds success.*

Great! Nice to know! But how do you get it if you haven't got it?

You know, it would be so easy to tell a struggling person, "All you need is a good dose of self-confidence". But it is quite another thing to tell them *how* to actually "get it". Think about it for a moment. Just how would you help someone acquire self-confidence? Would you say, "Just believe in yourself"?

Again, that sounds all flowery and nice, but it doesn't do a thing for that person *except* sound nice. We can't twist their arm and insist that they just "get" self-confidence. We can't *wish* it into existence. We can't get all excited, start jumping up and down, clapping our hands and singing zippy little songs and make it happen (like at one of those sales convention pep-rallies).

No, self-confidence can only come from within. And the best way to "get it inside of you" is for you to experience a victory—a success—a "*win*"!

The coach of a sports team can preach his heart out in the locker room before a game and have his players all whipped into a frenzy. But nothing, *nothing* can give self-confidence like a "win" can.

Since self-confidence comes from "winning at something", then how can you get that all-important victory?

Well, that is where the Three-Step/Jump-Start comes into the picture. It will give you a victory that will cause you to look at your circumstances and make you believe in yourself and in your abilities. You will see a tangible victory right before your very eyes!

So, are you ready? Then here it is: The "Three-Step/Jump-Start"

Step # 1. Get Up

Step # 2. Get Dressed

Step # 3. Make Your Bed

Now, you may be thinking, "What! That's it? I expected something a little more profound than that. Nothing that simple can be anything special?"

Well, if you thought that, you are right about one thing. It is simple. But if you think it isn't special; that's where you are mistaken. It is very special.

It is special because it gives you what your heart is crying for: Some very specific, very tangible victories in your life. These victories, in turn, heap self-confidence upon you.

And with this confidence you will begin to realize something amazing; there is almost nothing you can't accomplish in your life. It's a tall order, I know, but then again, confidence is a very powerful force.

21 Days

Now, this is the grueling part. The Three-Step/Jump-Start must be done for 21 consecutive days for it to become a habit. All three steps must be done, without fail, every single day. No exceptions, no excuses! (Short of sickness or death, that is).

So, in order to follow the three steps carefully, we will need to take a closer look at each one individually.

Step#1—Get Up

I know, I know. This sounds just way too easy because you already get up every morning, right? But, once you are up, do you *stay* up? Or do you secretly plan to slip back into bed for another 20 minutes of sweet slumber after everyone is out the door? If so…no, no, no!

Imagine yourself in a cross-country track meet. Once you've started the race and gotten a hundred or so yards down the track would you suddenly turn around and go back to the starting line. No! Of course not! It would completely stop your forward progress and, even worse, it would set you back. Once you've started the race, the only way to win it is to keep moving forward.

The minute you get are out of your bed, you have stepped into the race. Don't go back to the starting line!

Step # 2—Get Dressed

When you get up in the morning do you automatically reach for your bathrobe the very first thing? If so, do you continue to wear it throughout the morning, sometimes until the hour is approaching noon? I know I used to. I had a different bathrobe for every season. The thought of going from my pajamas directly into clothes sounded unnatural to me. It was like missing a step. But after learning that getting dressed was all a part of getting organized, I decided (reluctantly) to try it. Every single morning for the first 20 days it was like pulling teeth. It almost hurt. But by that mysterious 21st morning it actually *felt* normal. It seemed so *right* all of a sudden that I couldn't believe I ever thought it was acceptable to run around the house in my bathrobe all morning long. Yuck!

I frequently encounter women who say, "But I can't put on clean clothes without taking a shower first and there is no time for a shower first thing in the morning." Then they ask, "What should I do about that?" I sometimes think they are secretly trying to trick me into saying that it is OK to go ahead and put on their bathrobe in such a case. But I very sweetly and very calmly tell these ladies, "Then, put on yesterday's clothes until you have time for a shower. Or, put on a pair of sweats. Just *don't* wear your bathrobe."

Once in a while, one or two of these ladies will sigh deeply, letting me know that they don't agree with my position. But I can usually win them over with a couple of real life stories.

> **Note:** *For the past 20 years it has been my incredible privilege to teach hundreds of women the very principles I have written about in this book and I have been blessed beyond words to see their lives transformed by the power*

of organization. Some of my greatest blessings have come from women who have shared with me their own personal stories of how these principles have changed their lives. One lady named Jane shared her story of a harrowing experience that especially touched my heart...

———

Jane said she had gotten up this particular morning and had diligently gotten dressed—right down to her shoes. After breakfast she hugged and kissed her little girl good-bye then waited and watched at the window as her daughter crossed the street to catch the school bus. Jane watched in horror as a car, ignoring the flashing lights and stop sign of the bus, pulled out and drove around the bus, striking her daughter.

Jane said, "You wouldn't think that I would think of this at such an awful time, but I did. As I was riding in the back of the ambulance on the way to the hospital, it dawned on me how grateful I was that I was completely dressed, right down to my shoes, when the accident happened!" (By the way, her daughter miraculously suffered only minor injuries and recovered fully.)

Then there was another story told by a personal friend of mine, who happens to share my first name. Pat shared her saga in front of an entire room full of women who, at the time, were listening to me tell them that they should get up and get dressed first thing every single morning. Pat raised her hand and said that she could confirm that what I was saying was good idea. Her personal experience proved it.

Pat's thirteen-year-old daughter became quite upset one morning after she missed her bus for school. So Pat told her daughter, "No problem, dear. Calm down. I'll just drive you to school. Now, run and hop into the car." At the time Pat was wearing her bright pink bathrobe and big fuzzy slippers and her hair was going wildly in every direction. She didn't want to take the time to make herself presentable because her daughter was already running late. So Pat jumped into the car—just as she was—and drove her daughter to school. So far—so good. But after she turned around and started driving back toward home, she began to experience car trouble. Pat thought to herself, "Oh, my goodness, don't die! Not now! Not here! Not while I look like this!" She managed to coax her struggling car along for another mile or so before it finally sputtered to a stop and refused to start again. She barely managed to pull it off the side of the road. To make matters worse, it was pouring down rain. What was she to do? For the longest time, she just sat there, stunned and appalled that this was happening to her. The thought of looking under the hood to see what the problem was briefly flashed through her mind, but since she knew absolutely nothing at all about engines, she quickly dismissed the idea. She tried again and again to restart the car until it finally gasped its dying breath. She was stuck! She figured she would either have to walk home or wait until one of her family members eventually filed a missing person's report. She chose to walk.

She opened her car door, stepped out onto the wet street, and began the two-mile walk home, her fuzzy slippers collecting soggy, muddy road-dirt with each step. She was humiliated, angry with herself, and desperately hoping that no one she knew would see her in this predicament. She was determinedly marching along with her head down, her arms crossed in front of her, and mumbling sternly to herself when a loud horn suddenly blared behind her, startling her half out of her wits. She turned quickly and saw her next door neighbor in his big 4x4 truck. She gladly accepted the kind offer of a ride home but she said she never once glanced in his direction the entire trip.

She said it was a simply dreadful experience, but a lesson well learned. She told that room full of ladies that she has not missed a single morning of getting dressed immediately since that fateful day.

Any prior objections to my suggestion of getting dressed the very first thing in the morning usually vanish after I've shared these stories.

And why not? After all, it is for our own good. Because when we are dressed we are ready to start "playing the game" for real. And we are ready to start "winning" at that game, to boot. By contrast, when we slouch around in our bathrobe for hours on end, it is nearly impossible to muster the enthusiasm to get anything done.

This is the power of suggestion at work. *Getting up and getting dressed* is a check mark in the "win" column of our score sheet. It sends a powerful message to our subconscious. "You are a winner! You can do it!" But, *not getting dressed* is a check mark in the "lose" column. You don't feel confident. You don't feel capable of taking on the world because your brain doesn't have those wonderful victories to report to you. You feel blah!

For the minimum effort it takes to get dressed, you are greatly rewarded!

Step # 3—Make Your Bed

I imagine that moms who work outside the home would not have a problem with the first two steps of the Three-Step/Jump-Start. But when it comes to this third step, they may experience a bit of a melt down.

After getting up and getting dressed the very next thing you need to do is make your bed—immediately. Without exception. Well actually, there is *one* exception. That is if your husband is still in it. Otherwise you will end up with a rather unsightly lump in your bed. Of course, he probably won't be in bed all day, so that means as soon as he is out of it, you need to make it. Now, if your husband is a reasonable man (and I hope and pray he is), you can get creative and form an agreement with him. This is what Tom and I did. We made a legal and binding agreement between us (legal and binding because we shook hands on it) that whoever exits the bed last has to make the bed all by him- or her- self. I don't mean that if one person just barely makes it out of the bed before the other, then the loser has to make the bed alone. It isn't a race. What I mean is, if one of you gets up significantly before the other and has gotten dressed and moved on to other projects or activities, then the late riser has to make the bed alone.

Note of interest: *A bed that is made by two people is more than twice as fast to make as a bed made by one person alone. It saves all those trips you normally have to make walking backing and forth around it.*

Confession...I used to have a real problem with perfectionism where making a bed is concerned. If you will recall, my mother had taught me to make a bed with perfect hospital corners and covers so tight you could bounce a quarter off them. It would take me forever to make a bed. (Which may explain why I rarely ever bothered to do it.)

Tom, on the other hand, had never made a bed in his entire life before we got married. This made for an interesting combination. I would be standing on one side of the bed tugging and straightening the covers, one—at—a—time, until each was absolutely smooth and straight, while Tom was on the other side giving all the covers a heave simultaneously in the general direction of the headboard. He wore my patience thin and I'm sure I made his life miserable nagging and criticizing and insisting he do it… my way!

Then one day, something happened that made me question my rigid standards. Tom had slept in later than I had, so after getting up, he began making the bed all by himself (as per our agreement). I just happened to be walking passed our bedroom door at the time and saw him making the bed. Realizing he hadn't seen me, I quickly darted around the corner and peeked into the room to watch. I was curious to see if all of my diligent training had been paying off. What I witnessed made me weak in the knees.

He began by reaching across the bed from his side to mine. He grabbed the covers (all of them at once—sheets, blankets and comforter) and flung them toward the head of the bed. Then he did the same to his side—no needless steps around the bed several times for him! Next he wadded up our fluffy down-filled pillows into the shape of a basketball, stepped back a couple of steps, took careful aim and then threw them one at a time like an NBA player shooting free-throw shots. Swish! Nothing but net! I'll have to admit, they landed just exactly where they belonged. Next he tossed the sham-covered pillows and the other decorative pillows into place. Then he stood back and surveyed the finished product. The whole bed looked like a giant washboard. I knew that even he couldn't be happy with those results! And sure enough, I was right. He was clearly dissatisfied with the way it looked and immediately went to work to remedy the situation. *Good for him! I thought. He's finally catching on!* But before I could give myself a congratulatory pat on the back, he completely burst my bubble. He proceeded to vigorously pound out the lumps with his hands! It was such an appalling sight that I had to brace myself against the wall to keep from collapsing (you fellow perfectionists will identify with this feeling).

But do you want to know something even more appalling? When he was finished, the bed looked annoyingly good! Had I not witnessed it with my own eyes, I would never have guessed *how* the bed had been made.

That very day, I vowed to quit nit-picking at him when we made the bed together. Not to say that I planned to adopt his standards for myself, mind you, but at least I'd be more tolerant of his.

What I am trying to say here is this: If you want to get your husband's help with things around the house (like making the bed each morning) you may have to relax your standards a bit. If you are a perfectionist, it can hurt (believe me, I know) but in the long run, isn't having the help what you really want? Does it really matter that there are "pounded-out lumps underneath the covers"? And consider what is even more important, your relationship with your husband! So, relax! Don't nag. Keep sweet. And you will keep reaping all of those wonderful timesaving benefits of having the extra help.

So there you have the first *great* habit on your road to becoming organized: The Three-Step/Jump-Start. This is the habit that will start your engine and get you going each day! NO TURNING BACK!

CHAPTER 5

Great Habit #2

"ASAP"

I call the second great habit the ASAP habit. Of course, we all know what the letters stand for ...As Soon As Possible. Originally, I was going to call this the I-WOD habit... Immediately—With Out Delay. But I decided to go with the more familiar term. Either way, the meaning is the same. The more you can cultivate the habit of doing things "as soon as possible" or "immediately—without delay", the better off you will be.

In fact, the ASAP approach is so effective it could come with its own guarantee. A TV commercial advertising this habit could go something like this...

"Take the ASAP guarantee! It simply states: When you have a chore to do, try doing it as soon as possible. You will find it easier, quicker, and less demanding to do. Consequently, you will have more time to do the things you love. You will experience less frustration and anxiety and will enjoy the exhilaration and freedom that come from having accomplished something worthwhile. We are so sure you will love this product that we are making you this amazing

offer: Try it in your own home, 30 days risk free! If, after 30 days, you are not completely satisfied with the results, return it for a full refund."

We've all heard these kinds of advertisements. Some guy with a hyperactive personality and a piercing voice shouts the virtues of some wonderful product that will get out every stain known to man or remove even the toughest odor from our home. The guy with the annoying voice is so completely sold on his own product that we can't help but believe every word he says. And the first thing we know, we are running to the phone to order the product. Well, I don't have this man's flamboyant personality or his high-pitched, 90-words-per-second voice, but I am just as sold on my "product". And I think you will agree, once you give it a try!

The ASAP habit is such a valuable tool that you will wonder how you ever got along without it. Although it works well in all areas of your life, there are four household chores for which it is absolutely indispensable. It keeps them in check and prevents them from becoming "monsters". These are the ones I want to address. They are the dishes, the laundry, the mail, and the putting way of groceries (or other purchases) after a shopping excursion.

Eventually these chores will all have to be done anyway, right? Delaying doesn't change that fact. But when we delay, they become bigger, uglier, meaner and all the harder and more time consuming to tackle. It doesn't make one little bit of sense to delay, and yet, we so often do.

It is almost as though we have some "time-delay" mechanism built into us. We see a job that needs to be done, we know that we will, sooner or later, have to do it. We also know that the longer we put it off, the harder it will be to do. Plus, we know that until it gets done, we will have to live with the mess. Yet, in spite of it all, we still put it off. I think that down deep, we are pretty good con artists. We have convinced ourselves that if we ignore a job long enough it will somehow magically disappear. And since we didn't have to go to all the fuss and effort to do the job, we are "happier" because of it.

"Hello-o-o?" Are we really that gullible? Of course we are not *happier* when a job remains undone. I'm sorry, but try as we might, that job is *not* going to magically disappear. It will always remain in the back of our minds (if not in front of our very eyes) nagging at us, putting a guilt trip on us, and allowing us no pleasure or peace until the thing is done! Not to mention the fact that as the undone job just sits there, it grows, sometimes to almost insurmountable proportions. So, why not just do it and get it over with. Do it ASAP. Not only will the job be done and no longer hanging over our heads, but we will have the sheer joy of living in that cleaned up space instead of living *in* and having to deal *with* the mess. Believe me, *that's* what will bring true happiness.

I already mentioned one household chore that I had a hard time doing ASAP, and that was the dishes. Recently a young mother of two little boys e-mailed me asked, "What is the first step I should take to get organized?" I replied without hesitation, "Do your dishes immediately following each meal. Never wait until later to do them." Now, I have never been to this young lady's home. I've never seen the way she keeps house, but something I said must have hit a nerve. She shot back another e-mail, not quite indignant, but definitely flustered, and asked, "How do you know what my kitchen looks like? Have you seen it?" She thought for sure that I had some insider information as to the way her house looks.

No, I hadn't seen her house or her kitchen. But, as the old saying goes… I've been there, done that. And I know what *my* house looked like when I first began getting organized. Since she was desiring to get organized, I had a hunch that she was probably not terribly disciplined in her habits (since one leads to the other). And I knew that no matter what steps she took toward getting organized, they would be wasted if she wasn't *first* disciplined. So it was a necessary bridge to cross before we went any further.

Earlier, I mentioned the four areas that will benefit greatly from the use of the ASAP approach. There actually many, many more, but these four are so vital to our existence that they deserve a closer look.

The Dishes

Doing the dishes immediately following each meal will keep your kitchen looking nice all of the time instead of messy all of the time. Plus, it will get rid of that "monster" that follows you around pestering you, taunting you, and heaping coals of fire (a.k.a. guilt) upon your head.

When mealtime comes around, having the previous meal's dishes already done is an awesome feeling. If you are already in the habit of doing your dishes immediately following each meal, you will have a hard time understanding this feeling. But for those of us who haven't always followed this simple, yet profound, procedure the feeling it gives can come as a pleasant surprise.

And if, by some chance, unexpected company should drop by, what an absolute pleasure it will be to welcome them, joyfully and without hesitation, into your home. (You might even find yourself leading them *through* the kitchen on your way to the living room—even if it isn't the shortest or most direct route!).

Exceptions and balances: *This is hard for me to admit, to myself or to you, but I have a slight problem. I can easily confess that I was once a big-time slob. No problem. That's in the past. But what I must confess right now is very much in the present, and consequently very difficult for me to confess. Somewhere along the line, I let the pendulum swing too far in the other direction. Yes, I still declare that doing the dishes immediately following each meal is the right thing to do. Absolutely! But I now know that there can be exceptions to that rule. This exception actually becomes a rule in and of itself. And the rule is: "There are times when the dishes can wait." When you have company is one of those times.*

I have a question for you. When the rest of your family is sitting in the living room visiting with the guests in your home, is it better for you to be out in the kitchen doing the dishes or in visiting with your guests and family? This question is a painful one for me because I have been the one in the kitchen slaving away. Since I got my life organized, I've secretly had a deep-down fear in my heart. I fear that if I let anything slide, even for a moment (like the dishes), that I will revert back to my old ways, to my disorganized days. And that is a bondage that I will not go back into!

Finally, my Prince Charming, Tom, came to me one day and very gently challenged me to lay aside that fear. He wanted me to ignore the dishes the next time we had guests. He promised that he would help me get the dishes done after our guests went home. So, the next time we had guests for dinner, I stacked the dishes on the counter beside the sink and w-a-l-k-e-d away.

I sat and participated in the conversation, doing the best I could to enjoy the fellowship time we were having with our guests. All the while, Tom kept a wary eye on me, watching for signs of anxiety. Yes, to be honest, I did have a difficult time. I could actually see that stack of dishes from where I was sitting. But I didn't budge, not until our guests were in their car and pulling out of our driveway. As soon as they were out of sight, I made a mad dash for the kitchen. Tom, as per his promise, came along side and helped me. Just out of curiosity, I set a timer to see how long the clean up would take. When we finished with everything, right down to the wiping of the counter tops, Tom pushed the stop button on the timer and asked me to guess how long I thought it had taken. I guessed 33 minutes. He turned the timer around and showed me that it said...12 minutes!

All these years I had had that job blown out of

proportion in my mind. I had always thought that, by the time our company left, I would be too tired to do the dishes and that I would have to go to bed exhausted, leaving them undone. Then I would get up the next morning to that whole awful mess and then the breakfast dishes would be added to it and then the rest of the house would follow down that slippery slide as well. When in actuality, that was a completely unreasonable fear. (Isn't that how most fears are?) So, that is why I say, there can be exceptions to the ASAP rule. Keep your life balanced and keep in mind that people are more important than projects. (However, don't use people as an excuse to get out of doing your dishes ASAP on a normal, everyday basis. The main rule still is "Do them ASAP".)

The Laundry

Doing the laundry was always a fiasco for me. It was one of my weakest points! Looking back, I can now see *why*! Instead of using the ASAP method, I used the PIOUIBAN (Put It Off Until It Becomes Absolutely Necessary) method. Needless to say, that approach caused laundry day to be sheer torture for me.

But I've now learned that doing the laundry while it is still in its infancy stage keeps it from growing out of control. Simply put, I do more loads more often. This accomplishes a couple of things. It keeps the clothes hamper from bulging, straining at the seams, and overflowing the top. It also keeps our clothes clean and accessible to us more of the time. But most importantly, it makes the job far less intimidating. I used to struggle with getting the clothes from the hamper —all the way through the cleaning process —and back to the closets or dresser drawers without getting them hung up in the process somewhere along the line. And once they hit a snag, "zap"! The whole system broke down.

The most common place I experienced a hang up was at the *drying* stage. Once a load was dry, it became a stumbling block to me. Obviously, there were lots of items per load that now required personal, one-on-one attention. Up to that point, all of the items of clothing in one load could be dealt with as a clump. But once the load was dried, look out! That easy-to-handle clump was now separated and had become a whole bunch of individual items, demanding individual attention.

Logically, the easiest way to handle all of those items is to stuff them into a laundry basket and forget them. And, I guess for the moment, it is the easiest way. But in the long run that is a big mistake! *Can you guess how I know that?* Because that is the exact way I used to handle the dried load. Everything in the stuffed basket gets so badly rumpled that no one with a shred of dignity would be caught dead in them. So what does that mean, then? That they have to be ironed! Yes, ironed! When all I had to do was to remove them immediately from the dryer and hang them on a hanger! (Oh, the work I made for myself!)

It is inevitable. We WILL have to fold or hang those items of clothing at some point in time. Why not choose to do it now? Use the no-frills, no-gimmicks ASAP guarantee. It simply states that—when we do a chore ASAP, it will be much, much easier in the long run.

The Mail

Paper! It's one of the greatest clutter makers in our lives. And yet, who can resist the allure of running to the mailbox every single day. Usually, all it brings is junk mail, bills, and offers too good to be true. But there is always the remote chance that a piece of friendly mail might be tucked away in there somewhere. Or, who knows, we may even find an announcement that we've won some sweepstakes from somewhere that will change our lives forever. But, alas, it usually turns out to be just a pile of paper that we have to deal with.

But dealing with a pile of papers can be done anytime, right? It certainly doesn't have to be done as soon as we get back from the mailbox. And so, we set the pile down on the end of the counter and walk away to do other things. Three days later the pile is a little higher. And a month later the entire end of the counter is buried. And now, oh ugh! What a job it is to go through and sort that mess! Shoving needles under our fingernails sounds more appealing.

But, let's see if that whole pile can be *prevented* instead of *fixed*. When we use the ASAP approach, every single piece of mail is sorted, filed, and stored on the spot (either in the "to-be-paid" box, the newspaper or magazine rack or in the circular file). If there is a piece of mail that another member of the family needs to see, it is put in a special place specifically designated for that purpose. If we never, never, stack it on the counter or a table, then guess what. It never, never, becomes a "pile".

In the meantime, we enjoy a few other benefits from taking care of our mail ASAP. Bills don't get misplaced or forgotten so we don't get late charges or our electricity turned off abruptly. Invitations to parities or notices of upcoming events don't get overlooked causing us to miss out on all the fun. And joy of joys, our countertop looks neat and clean and can actually be used for other purposes—like preparing food!

The Groceries

A normal shopping day concludes with several trips from the car to bring in our many bags of groceries. We are exhausted from driving in heavy traffic to get to various stores around town to take advantage of this week's specials. Our feet ache, we are hungry, and we are weary to the bone. Somehow, just making it home and getting the groceries into the house feels like a triumph in itself. Who wants to even *think* about unloading all of those bags of groceries, and putting everything away?

And so we make ourselves a bite to eat, flop down in front of the TV and watch some mind-dulling program while we scarf down a sandwich and a few chips. Then we turn and face the piles of groceries, still patiently waiting for us to take care of them. Making a mental checklist, we poke around in the bags until we find the items that need to be refrigerated and put them away. Then we go to take a little nap.

After our nap, we are surprised to find that those groceries haven't put themselves away. So we give them one more chance. We go off to take care of some other business and before we know it, oops! It's time to start dinner for the family. Returning to the kitchen, we feel a little drop in our spirit as we see the groceries still waiting. But now, it's too late. There's no time to put them away. We have to start dinner!

We peel, dice, chop, fry and bake a lovely meal for our family, all the while dodging, shifting, and moving the groceries to make enough space for what we are doing. Before long, we sit down with our family and enjoy our meal. With a full, satisfied tummy, we get up from the table and go to do the dishes. But what we see shocks us. Our kitchen looks like a bomb has exploded in it. And at the bottom of the rubble heap—are all of those bags of groceries.

I know just how tired you can feel when you get home from a trip to town. I may even hold the world record for the shortest endurance when it comes to shopping. I get tired quickly and all I can think about is getting it over with and getting home. Once I'm home, I just want to be done. The last thing I want to do is put all of the groceries away.

But as much as I dread the job, I dread even more what happens when I don't. So now, when I bring home bag after bag of groceries, I literally force myself to put them away, ASAP. Sometimes, as I'm putting things away, I wonder why I bought so much stuff, but once the job is done, our cupboards are full, and the empty bags are folded and put away, I'm glad for everything I bought. And once again, I have proven to myself that the ASAP guarantee really works!

The next time you face one of these four obstacles in your life, just imagine me standing right there beside you yelling, "Come on soldier, get the lead out! I insist that you do the job right now, ASAP. You may hate me now, but you'll thank me later! Now snap to it or you'll have to drop and give me ten…and then guess what. You'll still have to do the job!"

Now, wouldn't it be easier to just do the job ASAP? Of course it would!

CHAPTER 6

Great Habit #3

"Taking Responsibility"

$\mathcal{T}$he third great habit is the Taking Responsibility habit. It simply means that you take full responsibility for yourself. This one habit will absolutely revolutionize your life. If you only take one principle from this entire book and plug it into your life—this is the one I would hope it would be. I'm not saying that the other principles aren't important, because they are! But getting this one ingrained into your life is the main thing that will make all of the other principles work!

Right now, if I could, I would shout it from the rooftops:

"Develop the Responsibility Habit and Your Battle is Half Won!"

Here's how it works. You must begin to TAKE FULL RESPONSIBILITY for every single thing you touch. Let me ask you a question. What is in your hands this very minute, the book that you are reading, right? What are you going to do with this book when you are finished reading it for the time being?

A. Set it down on the nearest tabletop

B. Leave it on the chair as you get up

C. Absent-mindedly drop it off somewhere on your way to wherever you happen to be going next

D. Make the effort to carry it to the spot you have designated as the place you leave books which you are currently reading (for example, on your nightstand or in a magazine rack)

The answer you give to this question will reveal a great deal about you and your unconscious habits. What will your habits dictate that you do? If you are in the habit of handling something then leaving it out, then look around you right now. What does your house look like? It probably looks like an explosion in a variety store. If you are in the habit of always putting every single thing away as soon as you are finished with it, then your house probably looks very neat and picked up right now. Once again, it is all about your habits.

You can probably guess where I am headed with this, right? Developing this habit means that you take responsibility for *everything* you use, touch, or handle. If you get something out, you put it away! It's that simple.

Let's just say that you're watching TV some evening and you decide that you want a snack. What do you do? If you are NOT in the habit of taking full responsibility—you go into the kitchen, open a cupboard, pull out a bag of munchies, put a handful into a bowl, and carry that bowl with you into the living room, right? Then, when you are done watching TV and ready to go to bed or move on to another activity, you get up and simply walk out of the room. If you are not in the habit of taking full responsibility for yourself, that is pretty much the way you would do it. But let's rewind a little and take a closer look at what that little activity would look like if you *were* in the habit of taking full responsibility for yourself.

The minute you finished putting the goodies into your bowl you would:

- Refasten the snack bag with a clip

- Put the bag back into the cupboard

- Close the cupboard door *before* leaving the kitchen

- Then, once you are finished eating your snack, you would take your empty bowl back into the kitchen
  Note: You don't have to jump up from your comfy spot and make a mad dash for the kitchen with your bowl the instant your snack is gone. Instead, you take it as soon as you get up for any other reason.

- Then you would put your bowl into the dishwasher—or, if you don't have a dishwasher, wash it, dry it, and put it away. And then, by all means, you would SHUT THE CUPBOARD DOOR!!!
  (Oops! Sorry about that little outburst there, but I have a thing about leaving cupboard doors open. It drives me to the brink!)

Do you see how this simple little principle just saved two items (your bowl and the bag of munchies) from being left out and becoming clutter?

But two items left out is the bare minimum. If you had a snack you probably also got yourself something to drink to go along with it. If it was a glass of cola, then the principle saved your dirty glass and the empty pop can from becoming clutter also. So now the Responsibility habit has saved a grand total of FOUR items from becoming clutter. BUT, if you take that number times the number of members in your family, just imagine how many items were saved from becoming clutter! It could easily be in the double digits!

Now imagine that each member of your family also participated in some sort of activity for the evening. It could be playing a video game, looking through your family photo album, reading a magazine, putting a puzzle together, or doing a homework project. Just imagine the number of items that could potentially be left out. Wow! It is staggering!

And now factor into the mix that, with bedtime fast approaching, there are baths to be taken. Towels, dirty clothes, shampoo, bathtub toys, toothbrushes, and toothpaste will be strewn from one end of the bathroom to the other. If no one in your family, including yourself, is in the habit of taking full responsibility for the things they wear, use, play with, or handle, then the results are inevitable. Your home is going to be overrun with clutter.

My dear, it is up to you. You must lead the charge. Unless you want to be a slave to your clutter for the rest of your life, you must begin to take full responsibility for yourself. (Then, after you have mastered the art, you can begin the very exciting, although challenging, process of training your family to do the same.)

> *Warning: Never attempt to do this in the reversed order. You must set the example, FIRST! If you tell your family to do one thing but you do another, they will see through you quicker than greased lightning. And then, you will have a full-scale mutiny on your hands. Do it the right way. Lead by example!*

And how do you do that? By going to war, that's how! You have to face and overcome the three main enemies of Responsibility. The are:

1. CARELESSNESS
2. ABSENT-MINDEDNESS, and
3. LAZINESS

These three little bad boys will march right into your home, flop down on your most comfortable furniture and absolutely take over your life. Every time you decide you are going to take a bold stand and make a positive change in your life, one of them will jump up and snatch away your determination. They are to be considered hostile and treated as the enemy. FIGHT! That's the only way to handle them.

Every time you see one of them show its ugly face, you punch him right in the nose, hard! Of course, in order to do that, you first must be able to recognize them. How? Through awareness training and discipline (oops, there's that word again). But don't sweat it, they are extremely easy to spot once you know what you are looking for them.

Carelessness

Carelessness is doing things haphazardly and without care. It is being nonchalant about your performance or actions and caring very little about the results. Of the three main enemies of responsibility, carelessness is the hardest to fight. That is because it is an attitude rather than an oversight. You can be made aware of an oversight and therefore can correct it. But how do you correct an attitude? The problem is if you don't care, you don't care. It is much easier to correct an oversight; it just takes a change of mindset. But to correct an attitude takes a change of heart.

If you think of your home as just a place to hang your hat, then how it looks probably doesn't matter to you very much. But if you see your home as a haven for you and your family, an oasis in a desert, a harbor in the storm, a place of warmth and hospitality, then you probably want it to be the absolute best it can be. *And* if you see your home as an extension of who you are, reflecting your tastes and style and revealing your innermost hopes and dreams, then there is even more reason to make it something special.

I guess it is all about perception. If your perception is that it doesn't matter how things look or how a job turns out, then you won't care enough to try to do your best. But if it *does* matter to you how things turn out, then you will be more apt to strive to do your best... in everything you do.

When you care, you are care-*full*. When you don't care, you are care-*less*. And carelessness leads to sloppy choices.

For example, when you change your clothes you are fully aware that there is now a set of clothes that you have just taken off lying on the bed or on the floor. It is not that you are *unaware* of that fact. You know good and well they are there. And you know that they don't look very tidy in that heap. But whether or not you pick them up and take care of them depends on if you care enough about your living conditions to make the effort. You see the problem is that caring requires action.

- After you use the phone book, what do you do with it?

- After you pay the bills, what do you do with everything you used (calculator, checkbook, stamps, payment stubs, etc.)?

- Once you've put on your make-up and done your hair, what do you do with all the items you used?

- When you and your family sit around the kitchen table and play a board game, what do you do with all the pieces when the game is over?

- After you brush your teeth, what do you do with the toothpaste cap, the toothpaste tube, your toothbrush, and the drinking glass?

Caring can only come from a feeling of self-worth. If you don't know your own value, then how can you care about anything else? If you don't have a spirit of caring, search your heart. How do you feel about yourself? If you find that you don't have a very high opinion, let me help you out. I happen to know that you are wondrously created and that you are highly valued, like a jewel of great worth. You (yes, you!) are so very special and you deserve the very best life has to offer. Once *you* recognize that fact you can begin to care about everything else in your life and carelessness will melt into carefulness automatically.

Absent-Mindedness

In order to spot absent-mindedness, you have to open your eyes, open your mind, and become fully aware of your actions. Unlike carelessness, we are usually not aware of the things we do absent-mindedly. So many of the things we do is so automatic that we don't even know we are doing them. How many times have you gone looking for something that you *just* had in your hand not more than 3 minutes ago? But now, somehow, it has vanished! If you try to remember exactly where it was that you released your grip on it—a mere 3 minutes ago—you're clueless. You have no recollection of that precise moment in time. Why? It is because you set it down while your mind was on something else.

But, if you were in the habit of *always* putting things away (not just putting them down) as soon as you were finished using them, then you would know exactly where that item would be found. In its proper place!

No more frustrating and often frantic searches for misplaced items. (I know some people who spend so much time searching for their car keys on a daily basis that it has cost themselves years of their life.)

Overcoming absent-mindedness is something you have train yourself to do. Every single time you pick something up, do some advanced thinking. Ask yourself, "What am I going to do with this when I am finished with it?"

Train yourself—train yourself—train yourself! Become aware of what your hands are doing. Frequently ask yourself, "What's in my hands right now and what am I going to do with it when I'm finished using it?" Making yourself AWARE is the key to winning this battle.

Have you ever watched a toddler with a toy? He will play with it until he sees a different toy that he wants instead. At that point, what becomes of the toy currently in his hand? He simply opens his hand and lets it fall. Then he makes a mad dash for the new toy he has set his sights on. It's as though the first toy ceased to exist the instant he spotted the other toy he wanted to play with. There was no conscious thought-process that caused him to reason, "Oh, wow! Look at *that* toy over there! It looks like more fun than *this* one. I want to play with *it* instead. I will set this toy down now so that my hands will be free to pick up that toy over there." No! He just let it go. It was out of his hand and out of his mind instantaneously. He may not even remember that the first toy ever existed.

I call this the "toddler syndrome". Unfortunately, most adults still have traces of the "toddler syndrome" in their lives to some degree or another. If you are one of them, you can, I repeat…you CAN overcome it. It's a matter of keeping your mind on what you are doing—*while* you are doing it. It means that you have to focus, focus, focus and think, think, think!

Laziness

I can hear it now, "I'd like to battle laziness, but I just can't seem to muster the energy". Ah, yes, this is a tough one to battle, because it involves getting off our derrières and doing the things we need to do at the times we need to do them. And if we are lazy, that is the last thing we want to do.

We want to have our cake and eat it too. We want to be able to do the fun stuff, but not take responsibility for the mess we made doing it. Before you bake that batch of cookies, realize that there is more to it than getting out all of the ingredients, measuring, mixing, scooping the dough onto the cookie sheets, and baking the cookies. Be aware that you must also wash every utensil, put away every ingredient, re-file the recipe card, wipe down the counter tops, and even sweep the floor if you dropped crumbs. If you are not in the mood to do it all, then don't start the project!

Overcoming laziness means that you have to finish your projects. No matter what you start, you have to finish it before you quit, even if that means you're down to the hard part. If you are working on your scrap-booking and you have gotten all the pages done that you set out to do, then you must clean up the "scrap" part of scrap-booking.

I've often wondered what was the difference between two of my friend's homes. One is neat, clean, and picked up most of the time (not perfect, but inviting). It is warm and comfortable and pleasing to be in. The other home is messy, cluttered, sometimes smelly, and almost always hectic. The respective mom's in charge of these two homes are close to the same age, of similar personalities, and have the same size families. So, what makes the difference? Why do they have such vastly different homes?

The only answer I can come up with is, simply stated: One *does* the work required to keep up her home and the other *doesn't*.

"Laziness" is one of the factors that could cause someone *not* to do the required work. I know, of course, that it is not the only thing; there could be any number of contributing factors. What you have to do is be honest with yourself. If you suspect that laziness is playing a part in your life and is dragging you down, then it is time to "go to the gym" and get yourself in shape. Do your jumping jacks and your sit-ups. Get rid of the flab! When you see something that needs to be done, get up and go do it! Take charge! Refuse to allow yourself to kick back and take it easy when there is a job to be done. It will take a degree of sweat and toil, but as your muscles develop, laziness will have to take a hike!

Review

Being lazy, careless, or absent-minded doesn't save us from having to work! Oh, sure, for the moment it does. But down the road, it only creates *more* work for us. Because we will eventually feel the need to clean the pigsty that we, with the help of our family, have created. And, oh brother, will it ever be labor-intensive when we do.

It is a simple concept: Keeping things up as you go—saves you work in the end. Letting things get out of hand, always, always costs you extra work because—

When you live like a pig,
You have to work like a dog!

You deserve better than that! And I know you can make it happen. I believe in YOU!

Practice Patience

These three great habits, the Three-Step/Jump-Start, ASAP, and Taking Responsibility, are essential qualifications for becoming a truly organized person. I'm sure some of you are thinking, "All I want is to get my closets organized! Why all this annoying talk about *habits* and *discipline*? Please, just get to the closets! The rest of this is a waste of time!"

To anyone who would say that, I would answer, "I know how you feel. You are anxious to see the end results. You want to skip directly to the finish line. You want to jump over all the middle stuff and just get the job finished so you can be done with it. I understand."

You see, I am the same way. I am the most impetuous person in the world. I want what I want when I want it. I certainly don't want to have to wait for it. But I am learning (very slowly) that patience yields great rewards. I'm also learning that instant gratification can be very hollow.

Believe me, if there were a shortcut to true organization, I would have told you about it FIRST—before anything else. Yes, of course, you *could* skip to the end. You could just start opening closet doors and organizing all the stuff inside them, but you wouldn't be happy with the results, not for very long, anyway. It would be a hollow victory because it would—not—last.

I know that the route I am urging you to take is the slow way, but it is the sure way. It is the way that will produce lasting results. And it is the *only* way that will change *you* and not just your stuff.

This training period is your "boot camp". Of course, we all know that boot camp is always tough. There's no doubt about that. But when you graduate, you will be a genuine, bonafided, well-trained, lean, mean, organizing machine. Like I said before, you will battle clutter, chaos, confusion, and disorder and you WILL win!

Thinking Ahead

Just imagine what your house is going to look like once you have developed these habits in your life. And then, oh my goodness, imagine what it will be like once you get your family trained to do the same. *What? You didn't know that you had to do that? You thought once you graduated Boot Camp that the battle was over, the war was won.*

Sorry, soldier. That's not the way it works. You get through the rigors of Boot Camp, you earn your stripes, and then YOU become the Drill Sergeant. That's the way it works! Otherwise, you end up fighting the whole war all by yourself. Who ever heard of a soldier winning a war all by himself? It just can't happen. You need the whole army fighting with you. And no army is capable of fighting and winning without FIRST being trained for combat.

Once you get those little recruits of yours trained, you just won't believe the difference it makes. It's the stuff dreams are made of! Your workload will be slashed, and your house will be in better shape than ever before! It sounds like an oxymoron, doesn't it? But let me assure you, it will happen!

CHAPTER 7

To Train, or Not to Train? What a Silly Question

*O*nce you have *made* progress, you're going to want to *keep* the progress that you've made. And now that you are taking full responsibility for yourself, much of your battle has already been won. But, if your family is still living in a fairy-tale land where they think little elves come in and do all the cleaning up after them, then you are still stuck in that land with them. And guess what that makes you—the little elf!

Is that how you want to live your life? Doing *everything* for your family, *all* of the time? If so, then I am here to tell you—STOP THAT!

You may think you are just loving them, protecting them, and serving them when you insist on doing all of the work yourself, but that is not the case. In fact, what you are really doing is *cheating* your family. You are cheating them in two ways:

#1. You are keeping them from learning valuable life-lessons in responsibility, accountability and capability.

#2. You are depriving them of your best!

I can hear it now. Some of you are saying, "What? What do you mean, I'm depriving them of my best? I am *giving* them my best when I do all these things for them! How can you say such a thing?"

Easy. Because it's true. When you run around behind them picking up the things they so flippantly leave behind, and clean up all of the messes they so thoughtlessly make, you are using up all of your "bests" just to clean-up and pick-up after them.

You're wasting your best energy…time…emotions…love…attentions, etc., etc., when you could have used those "bests" to shower them with words of kindness and wisdom. Love and laughter. Compassion and kind (but firm) correction. And T-I-M-E! Time to sit and just listen to their hearts. Time to talk. Time to play games. Time to hug. Time to BE THERE for them and with them. Time *and* energy to bake cookies for them…and with them. Time to be together. Time, time, time. Precious time.

But if you are so busy cleaning up after them, there is no time (or energy) left for the most wonderful things in life. And when you do give them something of yourself, it is often your frustration, exasperation, and resentment. How sad! What a waste!

You can actually give *more* to your family when you *don't* make yourself a slave to them. And you can give more to others outside your four walls as well.

And don't forget about yourself! Mothers often feel that they are being selfish when think of themselves. They say things like, "I feel guilty when I think of my own needs. Isn't it every mother's duty to think of her family first and foremost."

I'm sorry, but I don't buy that! Yes, of course, I believe that you should be a devoted, loving, caring, nurturing mother (*and* wife). But don't become so absorbed in your devotion to your family that you forget that you, too, are a human being with needs (physical, mental, emotional, and spiritual). You have to make time for YOU! It is imperative! Otherwise you will suffer "burnout". And then what good will you be to anyone else? You need to be renewed, refilled, and refreshed…often. Not just for your own sake, but for the sake of your family also.

Where To Start

You start by *training* your family to take full responsibility for themselves. Now, this has to be done with extreme caution. If you were to suddenly go from being everyone's personal slave to being on strike and making them fend for themselves it would be like leaving a fish flopping on the ground and telling it, "You find your own way back to the water."

You have to begin slowly. You have to begin by patiently teaching, painstakingly instructing, and slowly relinquishing control over the areas of their lives where you are training them. It is not an overnight process. Responsibility takes time to instill. That's for sure. But if you never begin…it will take even longer.

This training benefits both you and your family! It is a win/win situation.

So what are you waiting for? You have nothing to lose and everything to gain. The answer to the question, "To train or not to train?" has been definitively answered. By all means…TRAIN!

So, what do you say? Shall we get that precious little family of yours whipped into shape? Remember: It is for their own good. It's for your own good. And it is for the good of everyone else, including society at large.

CHAPTER 8

Drill Sergeant "Mom"

Oh, brother! If you thought Boot Camp was tough for YOU! Just wait until you start training all of those new recruits of yours. But take heart. It will be so well worth it once they are trained, responsible, and conscientious that you will never regret the time or effort you devoted to the task. The value to *you* will be immeasurable. But what is even more important is how valuable this training will be to *them!* For your children, it will be something they will carry with them throughout the rest of their lives. You will be instilling in them responsibility, accountability, and capability. These qualities will help form and shape their very character. What an absolutely priceless gift you will be giving them! Believe it or not, this training will be as valuable to them as their diploma will be!

Will it be tough? Sure it will! (So was childbirth, but you gladly went through the ordeal for the prize at the end). Remember this: Anything worthwhile will cost you something. But with a little creativity, you can make the job a whole lot easier.

Note: When you begin to train your family, you are going to need to become one tough drill sergeant. That's the way you will instill them with discipline. But, what you don't want to do is simply create robots who fear you and follow your orders without questioning a word you say. Your true goal in all of this should be to train your children to someday stand on their own, to be able to take initiative, and to be self-motivated. In the meantime, you will reap the side benefit of having a considerable amount of extra help around the house from these leaders-in-training.

So, in the training of your family, you want to be sure to give them the knowledge they need to be able to "fish" for themselves, not just to follow orders. Am I saying that obedience is not important? Oh, my goodness, no! Do you have the right to expect obedience from your children? Absolutely! In fact, you had better expect it. But, obedience without knowledge is slavery. So, in your training, you need to continually keep in mind that you are not just training "helpers" for yourself, you are training future adults. And you want them to be fully functional, efficient, diligent, responsible, reliable, and competent.

So, you have to teach them to *understand*, not just *obey*. Now, here is your challenge—to become a tough drill sergeant—but at the same time, a sweet one who *teaches*…not just *commands*. Does that sound impossible? I guess it kind of does, doesn't it? But I believe with all my heart that it IS possible. *How*, you ask?

Ah, well now, that's where you have to get a little creative. Wouldn't it be nice if you could begin to train your family without them even knowing they are being trained? Wouldn't it be fun if their training could look and feel more like a *game* than a regimented training program? Well, believe it or not, it can!

Where to Start,
When the Task Looks Overwhelming

When my children were small, our family could have applied to the Federal Farm Bureau for tax credits and probably have been granted those credits quite liberally because, in all honestly, we lived like a family of pigs. I desperately wanted order in my home. But it's tough to have order when you are clueless about the causes and effects of *disorder*.

Then one day I began to develop the habit of Taking Responsibility in my life. It wasn't easy. I was such a "master of messiness" that everywhere I went I left a trail of odds and ends behind me in my wake. But then I started working to overcome this habit of sloppiness in my life and I refused to quit until I had won the battle. When I finally did win, it was an awesome feeling!

But then, low and behold, it was time to train my family. The problem was, they had *already* been trained! They had been trained by *me*—the master of messiness! And I had done a pretty good job of it, too, if I do say so myself! I had taught them to follow my example—and wouldn't you know it, they learned like true champs. Everywhere they went (just like I had taught them), they left a trail of stuff behind them. Oh, my goodness! How would I ever be able to *re*-train them? Not a one of them had a single ounce of responsibility coursing through their veins.

I didn't know where to start. I knew that if I suddenly started making strict rules, demands, and requirements they would suffer culture shock. Their brains would be instantly fried, as if struck by a bolt of lightening. A picture formed in my mind of the three of them in frizzy hair with smoke curling up from it. I wanted to train them without toasting them. But how?

Well, believe it or not, the answer came in the form of a game. It was a simple little game, actually, but an extremely effective one. The minute (yes, the minute!) we started playing the game, things began to change for the better.

The Changes

In my wildest dreams, I could never have imagined the changes this game would bring about in our home and family. All that I had dared to hope was that it would help our house look less cluttered and messy. What actually happened was so much more.

A sense of peace and joy began to settle in our home to a degree that we had never experienced before. Stress and anxiety started to melt like snow. My mood was changing because I was spending less time picking-up after everyone or constantly bickering at them to do it. I began to feel like a different person, a nicer, kinder one. My family began to respond to the "strange" woman in their home by becoming kinder and sweeter themselves. Wow! And to think, it all started with a little game!

It happened for us. It can happen for you.

So put on your combat fatigues, you tough, amazing, sweet, little drill sergeant moms, and let the games begin!

CHAPTER 9

The Dime Game

$\mathcal{W}$ell, here it is…the game that started it all. The game that launched my family on a journey into a bold new world. A journey into the world of *responsibility*. It was a scary new world to them at first, but they soon got used to the idea. And before long, there were amazing transformations taking place before my very eyes.

This game was not the end of my family's education, to be sure. But it was a wonderful starting place. Remember this: Education is progressive. Your children will learn, just as they do in school, a little each day.

The beauty of this game is that it will open the eyes of every member of your family. It will make them keenly aware of when they are leaving things out—instead of putting those things away where they belong. But it will do even more than that. It will actually make them anxious *not* to leave those things out. *Impossible, you say?* Oh, ye of little faith. Read on…

Introducing…"The Dime Game"

The dime game is designed to make every member of the family aware of their actions and to train them to take responsibility for themselves. It does this by bringing their sloppy habits to their attention. The game is based on one simple principle: The principle of "rewards and consequences". It is called "THE DIME GAME" and is played with (what else) …dimes. Lots and lots of them.

Note: Now, let it be according to your budget. When our children were small, we used dimes, which is why we called it the dime game. But in today's economy you may be able to play with a higher denomination of coins. You may even be able to play with dollar bills! But then again, maybe you can only play with pennies. When one of these is the case, the game would then be called the PENNY, QUARTER, OR DOLLAR game. Whichever you choose to use will determine the name of your game.

What You Will Need

Fortunately, this game is simple, requiring only a couple of "game pieces" in order play. Those pieces are: coins and containers for those coins. The coins are to be allocated ten to each member of the family, each week. These coins are to be put in separate containers, one for each player of the game. (Hint: Baby food jars work well.) Of course, if you are blessed enough to be playing the DOLLAR game then you may want to use envelopes to keep them in.

Each container is then labeled with the name of one member of the family, until every member has a jar with his or her name on it. This includes *every* member of the family, including mom and dad. (Everybody plays!)

These jars of coins are to be kept in one central location throughout the duration of the game. They can be lined up across your fireplace mantel, on a windowsill, on a desktop, or wherever you choose.

Weekly Rotation

The game is played on a rotation basis, one week at a time. At the end of one week, the game culminates and then *immediately* begins again for the next week. At the beginning of each new week, all players begin the game with a fresh new start, on an equal basis, and with a new set of ten coins.

Object of the Game

There are two distinct objects of this game.

1.   The first is to try to keep from loosing any of the coins
     allocated to you at the beginning of each new week. There
     is only one way that this can be accomplished. And that is
     by *taking full responsible* for the everything you use, touch,
     or handle. That means that you have to put everything
     away—where it belongs—as soon as you are finished using
     it. Otherwise it becomes a violation and can be "captured" by
     other players of the game.

2.   The second objective is to attempt to catch other members
     of your family in the act of failing to put away something
     that they have used, touched, or handled. This second
     objective keeps everyone on their toes.

Rules Of The Game

The rules of the game are simple. The first rule is this: You are not allowed
to leave anything out which you have used. When you are finished using an
item, you must put it away…where it belongs. You are not allowed to leave
it out or to absentmindedly lay it down somewhere. That includes anything
and everything that you get out to use for any purpose whatsoever (to look
at, read, play with, wear, eat from, write with, listen to, curl your hair with,
dry your body with, brush your teeth with, etc., etc., etc.). When you are
finished using an item, you must put it away.

The second rule is: If you *do* leave something out and it is caught by some
other player you must first put that item away and then you must pay a fine
for that item. The fine amount is…one coin from your coin jar. This is the
"consequences" portion of the game.

Variations

Every family is different. What works for one, may not work for another. Therefore, you need to tailor the game to fit your family's personality. Here are three variations of the dime game from which to choose. (You may be able to think of even more ways to play. You are only limited by your imagination!)

Variation #1. Each player competes only against himself.

- **In this version, coins that are lost by a player are put into a common "kitty". The goal of each player is to loose as few coins as possible by the end of each week.**

Variation #2. Each member of the family directly competes against every other member of the family.

- **In this version each player attempts to keep as many of his own coins as possible while at the same time trying to add to his stash by catching violators and requiring a coin from their jar which they must pay as a fine.**
- **At the end of the week, the player with the most coins wins.**

(Note: The finder of a misplaced item should never be allowed to extract a coin from anyone else's jar. Only the person who owns the jar should be allowed to remove coins from his or her jar. That does not mean, however, that the violator has a choice whether or not to pay a fine. When you get caught, you pay!)

Variation #3. Teams are formed and then teams compete against teams.

- **In this version, teams can be made up of parents against the kids, boys against the girls, or any other combination.**
- **The team with the most coins at the end of the week wins.**

Setting the Stage

On the morning of the day that you plan to launch your game, get your coins counted out and put into the "labeled" jars. Then, before everyone leaves for school or work, tell your family that you have a little surprise for them. Show them the jars with the coins in them. You can even pick one up and shake it back and forth gently. The clinking sound the money makes is a great attention grabber (just ask anyone who has ever been to Las Vegas.) Then tell them that you are planning to play a fun, new game with them (involving these jars of money) and that you will begin the game as soon as everyone gets home later today. If they try to weasel any more information out of you about game right then, heighten their curiosity a little by saying, "Sorry, I can't tell you any more right now. You'll just have to wait".

Underwhelm Them

You and I both know where this game is headed. The ultimate goal of the game is to teach responsibility to each and every member of your family, in all areas of their lives. But, let's face it, that is simply TMI (Too Much Information) for your family to handle at this point. That is why this must be kept a well-guarded secret. If they even suspected that that was the ultimate goal of the game, they would experience overload to the brain and would be fried on the spot.

If, however, you release tiny bits of information at a time, they can accept and assimilate it slowly, and will learn and grow as a result.

You must also release only tiny amounts of *expectations* at a time as well. You simply cannot expect too much of them too quickly. So, START SLOW. *Under*-whelm them instead of *over*-whelming them.

How, you ask? By starting the game with only "one" room of the house. I like to suggest that it be your living room or family room (wherever your family spends the most time).

Preparing the Room

On your launch day, you will need to have that room completely ready to start the game. That means that it must be picked up thoroughly with *nothing* left out of place. If the room is a huge mess, don't even attempt to start the game! It would be disastrous. Even if the room is only a little messy, don't start the game! It needs to look like a "show room" on the day that you launch the game! Once you have gotten everything picked-up, then be sure to vacuum the floor and dust everything in sight. Even if it means that you have to spend the entire day getting the room ready to play the game, that's OK. Do whatever it takes. You must start the game with a deliciously clean room.

Starting the Game

The game starts for each person the second they walk through the door as they arrive home from school or work on the day that you launch your game. To introduce the game, you need to catch them at the door—before—coats and shoes come off and books, papers, and lunch boxes go flying in all directions.

Catch them at the door and tell them something like, "Do you remember the game I told you about this morning? Well, the game is starting…right now. This very minute. So, hang up your coat, put your shoes away, empty your lunch box in the kitchen, and put your school books in your room and then come into the living room and I will explain the game to you. Hurry now, I can't wait to get going."

If you are not normally in the habit of making them take responsibility for their coats and books, etc., I guarantee you that they will look confused. They may even be a little leery, wondering what on earth you're up to. Regardless of how they behave, don't react to them. You've got to be upbeat. You need to present the game as fun and exciting.

When they finally do join you in the living room, their mouths may drop open at the sight of such a bright, clean, beautiful room (especially, if it isn't normally that way). At this point you can say something like, "Doesn't this room look beautiful?" When they agree with you, you can add, "Don't you wish it could always look like this?" (You're throwing out a little bait for them, here.) When they *bite* you can say, "Well, guess what, it can! The game that we are going to play will KEEP it looking this way…all of the time! Doesn't that just sound like too much fun?" (About now would be a good time to rub your hands together vigorously and grin from ear to ear to show your excitement.)

Now they will really look confused! They're thinking *Monopoly, Sorry,* or *Uno* and wondering how any of these games will help the living room stay neat and pretty.

"No, it isn't *Monopoly, Sorry* or *Uno,*" you can explain. "It isn't an actual board game that we are playing, but in a way, it kind of is. There are game pieces, rules, and even a game board."

Go on to explain that the *game pieces* are the little jars of coins that you showed them that morning. (You might want to show the jars again at this point. You can even let each person hold his own jar while you explain the game.) Then explain that the *game board* is this room. Tell them that any time they enter this room, they are automatically "playing the game". There are three basic rules of the game.

Explain the Rules of the Game to Your Family

The three basic rules of the Dime Game are:

#1. When you set foot into this room, you are automatically playing the game. Even if you decide that you don't want to play, forget it…you are still playing. The choice is not yours. If you somehow manage to forget about the game, you are still playing. Forgetting does not excuse you from the game. If you *do* forget, someone will be there to gently remind you that the game is still in progress—(probably by relieving you on one of your coins!)

#2. Anything and everything that you bring into this room becomes YOUR responsibility. You are the one who is responsible to put it away when you are finished with it. There are no exceptions.

#3. If you *don't* put it away, you must pay a fine. The amount of the fine is one coin from your coin jar.

Note: It is important that you stress the point that everyone in the family is playing the game, including mom and dad. (To prove your point, you can show them that there are jars with your names on it as well.)

Fair Game

If, when you are finished using an item, you fail to put that item away, that item becomes "fair game" and can be "captured" by any other member of the family.

That brings up a great question. What actually constitutes "fair game" and what does not? There is the potential for a slight case of "war" to break out here if one player becomes a tad bit over zealous, trying to capture something that has not actually become fair game yet. If, for example, you are sipping a cup of tea and set the cup down on the end table beside you in between sips, that cup is NOT fair game.

If one of your children is doing his homework in the middle of the living room floor and gets up to go to the bathroom, that homework is NOT fair game. If, however, he gets up and goes to bed and leaves his books and papers all sprawled out on the floor…then it IS fair game.

I'm sure you get the idea. Now all you have to do is teach it to your family. It is a bit of a balancing act. But, don't worry. They will get the hang of it. Trust me, they will!

Capturing

An item that has been left out is "captured" when it is discovered by another member of the family. That person (the discoverer) points out, to the person who left it out, the fact that the item was left out. At that time, the first thing the person who left the item out must do is to take care of the item. (He or she must put that item away... where it belongs. He or she is not allowed to simply move it beyond the borderline of the game.) Then the perpetrator must take one coin from his or her own jar and give it to the discoverer. The discoverer then takes that dime and puts it into his jar. (Note: The discoverer is not allowed to simply pocket the money. That money is still "in play" and can not be claimed until the game closes at the end of each week.) (Also: The discoverer is not allowed to go to the perpetrator's jar and get the money himself. The only person allowed to take money from a jar is the owner of that jar.)

Note: This brings up an interesting point. What if the perpetrator refuses to pay the discoverer? I can certainly see this happening among siblings. That's where you, (drill sergeant, mom), come in. You must moderate the game. Keep it fair and keep everyone playing with honesty and integrity.

And by all means, moms and dads, when you get caught (note I said when not if), you should never be reluctant to pay the piper. It is good for the kids to catch you once in a while. They will be so excited when they do. And when you hand over that coin from your jar, they will beam. This will keep their interest for the game high.

Cashing In

At the end of the week, it is time to "cash in". With you acting as moderator, everyone gets to empty his or her jar and keep the coins that are left in it. Some people will have fewer coins than they started with and others will have more.

Once the jars have been emptied, you must refill them right away for the coming week. (Remember when I said that anything worthwhile will cost you something? Well, this is where you "pay up". Refilling those cars can be expensive. But think of it as the cost of education. But even more than that, think back to how great the game kept that room of your house looking. That is worth its weight in gold.) So, don't begrudge the money as you put it into the jars. Sing and dance as you fill them. Let your heart rejoice for all that is being accomplished with these few little coins.

Running Out of Coins Before Week's End

What if someone is so sloppy that he or she runs out of coins before the end of a rotation? Do they just "sit out" the game for the rest of the week?

No! No one is allowed to "sit out". If they were, they may run out of coins intentionally so that they won't have to play. That is a big no-no! That is where a penalty phase of the game must be instituted.

Penalties

If a player runs out of coins before the end of a game and continues to commit violations, he or she must be penalized. These penalties can be creative and varied. Remember: Let the punishment fit the crime. Assigning extra chores (of approximately a five or ten minute duration) is a very fitting penalty. But whenever a penalty must be paid, it does not alleviate the perpetrator from FIRST having to put away the item that he or she originally left out. This is "in addition to" not "instead of".

Expanding the Game

Once you have gotten comfortable playing the game in that one room of your house slowly begin to incorporate other rooms. But, of course, ONLY after they have been cleaned to a spit-shine first. And, may I suggest, that you move slowly as you expand to other rooms, perhaps only adding one room per week. And, when you *do* add a room, you must make it very clear that that new room is "on" the game now. (Don't go retroactive.)

Your family will have a very clear sense of where the game is being played and where it isn't. If your family is like mine, you will be able to see a clear dividing line between rooms that are "on" the game and those that are not. It can be quite comical. It is like a line drawn in the sand. On one side of the line is complete order and beauty. On the other side it looks like an F-5 tornado just blew through. But, don't become overly concerned about the areas of the house that still look like a war zone. Those areas will come around as the game expands. And before you know it, your whole house will be "on".

How Long To Play

How long you play the game is up to you. It will depend greatly on your family. Eventually, the game will begin to subside. As your family learns to take responsibility, the need for the game decreases.

You may let the game fade out and then, a few weeks or months down the line, notice that everyone seems to be getting a little sloppy in their habits again. If that happens, all you have to do is resurrect the game. Everyone will already know all the rules so it will be very easy to swing right back into the game for a period of time.

You will most likely find that you are the only one who will ever instigate the game. So, that is why I say that how long you play the game is up to you. You are the one who can judge how well your family is doing and will make your decision based on that information.

Whatever you do, keep it lively. Keep it fun. And keep it going as long as there is a need for it. You will reap great rewards for your diligence.

Not The End

Like I've already said, this game is only the beginning of your family's education in the area of responsibility, not the end. You will teach them many, many more things as you go along. It is kind of like when you are teaching your children *good manners,* you may start with please and thank you, but you surely wouldn't stop there. You would teach them not to interrupt, to look people in the eye when they talk to them, to chew with their mouths shut, etc.

The same is true when teaching them to be responsible. The dime game could be compared to "kindergarten", it is great place to start, but there are still grades 1-12 to go.

You may never have thought of yourself as a teacher of higher education, but you really are! It may be tough, and there will be days when you wonder if anything you are doing or saying is even getting through. But don't become discouraged. Don't give up. You ARE making a difference. If you will remain diligent in your training and patient in your instruction, your children WILL most definitely learn responsibility. They won't be able to help themselves.

CHAPTER 10

Work Smarter—not Harder

At the same time that your family is going through their formal education, you can be gaining your degree in higher learning right along with them. Your education into the bright and wonderful world or *Organization* doesn't stop with the development of some super-duper habits and the training of your family, rather it just begins there.

The next levels of learning will take you even higher and then higher until you get up some morning and realize that you don't even recognize yourself any more. You will be one bold, confident, dynamic, mamma! Ready to take on new challenges, to grow to new heights, and to step out into areas that would have been inaccessible to you before.

So, shall we move right along? Of course, we shall! Because you are so ready for it!

Once you and your family have developed the habit of taking full responsibility for the things you use, touch, and handle, your home is going to be much easier to clean on a daily basis. Now all that is left to do is to take care of the mess that "life" makes. Life is just messy. You know that, don't you? There's no way around that fact, no matter how diligent you are. Certain precautions can help diminish or lessen their severity, but for the most part, they just happen. Dust settles, dirt gets tracked in, soap scum builds up, leftovers collect in the refrigerator, dishes get dirty, spills and splatters...splat.

It just happens. You can't stop it. But you *can* clean it up!

And would you believe, not all cleaning routines are created equal? There are good ways, better ways and there are best ways to clean. Not to mention the fact that there are also some really *bad* ways.

In my pre-organized days, the method I used to clean my house could have been classified as one of the really bad ways. I cleaned by using the triage method.

Note: "Triage" is the system used by the medical profession to determine who gets medical attention first at the scene of an accident or in the emergency waiting room of a hospital (or in wartime, on the battlefield). This entire decision making process is based on one thing—urgency. Those people whose life depends on quick treatment are put at the head of the line and treated before those whose injuries are non life-threatening.

This whole triage thing seemed like a pretty good idea to me so I borrowed it from the medical profession and applied it to my house cleaning routine. That means that I did the most urgent things first, then the things that seemed less urgent second, third, fourth, and so on down the line. By the way, the things that seemed least urgent seldom ever got done at all.

Included in this triage method of cleaning was a random, usually _frantic_, picking up of items that had been left out of place. In our house, there were always so many of these items that the bulk of my cleaning was made up of "picking-up" and "putting-away". After all, it was the most obvious, the most "life-threatening" need at the time. Consequently, the picking-up stage of cleaning was *always* my first priority. It was the thing that was the "most urgent" and the thing that daily got triaged to the front of the line.

I didn't have a plan or a strategy for getting "everything else" done. I simply couldn't see past the clutter. Once things were picked-up, my house looked so good compared to the way that it did before I started picking-up that it seemed and felt as though my work was done. My mission was accomplished.

"Picking-up"

I remember one day as I was beginning my morning ritual of "picking-up", I decided to keep a tally of how many items had been left out by each member of my family. That way I could show everyone just *why* I had to work so hard every day and just *who* the guilty parties were. As I started working, a little speech began to churn around and form in my mind. It was a glorious little speech, designed to bring remorse and regret to the perpetrators. If the speech was powerful enough and the guilt-trip I was going to put on them compelling enough, they might just shape up and stop leaving stuff out all of the time. It was worth a shot, anyway.

At the end of the day when my tally was complete, I kept my big mouth shut. Because—*I won!* I was the guiltiest of us all! (I didn't see that one coming.) That does not mean, however, that the other members of my family were blameless. To the contrary! Every single one of us was guilty! (Just some more than others.)

And so my "picking-up" blues continued, day after day. It seemed as if the entire purpose of my life revolved around it. How sad! That's like working your tail off just to make it to the starting line of a race. But the saddest part of all was that making it to the starting line felt like "winning" the race to me. And so often, that was the exact point where I quit working (pleased as punch with myself for all that I had accomplished). Never mind that the dust was piling up so thick you could plant potatoes in it, or that you could barely see out the windows, or that the burner trays on the kitchen stove were completely encrusted with a two-inch thick layer of burned-on food. Those things were hardly noticeable to me. All that mattered was the surface stuff. And once that was accomplished, YIPPEE! I was done. I was free. I was—exhausted! (Usually, there wasn't enough time or energy left to accomplish anything beyond that point.)

Confession Time: When my children were quite young, it was a rare occasion when I actually got completely done—even with just the "picking-up" portion of the cleaning process. It was like being on a merry-go-round. By the time I made it back to the place where I had started, there was already another mess needing to be cleaned. I'm quite certain it had something to do with the fact that I had a little band of merry-makers following right behind me undoing what I had worked up a pretty good sweat to do in the first place. (Mothers of preschoolers will identify with this.)

So, as you can see, my method of choice for cleaning my house, triage, was not the best. That, together with the lack of responsibility within our family, made for disastrous results. However, once we got the responsibility issued under control, that left only my "cleaning method" in desperate need of repair.

Where cleaning is concerned, there is one thing, one simple, remarkable concept that I never considered before. Like I said, I had only used the triage method. Basically, I looked around, saw what needed to be done, and virtually attacked it. But never—no never—did I ever PLAN my cleaning. I look back now I think, "Duuuh"! It is so logical that it blows my mind. But for some strange reason, back in my pre-organized days, it just never occurred to me!

The Power Of Planning

I've now learned that there is power in planning. I've learned that plotting your course before you ever start, will save you hours of unnecessary backtracking.

If you were taking a cross-country trip, you certainly wouldn't jump in your car and just start driving without planning your course, would you? Of course not! Because you know that the success of your trip is directly related to the excellence of your plan.

In the same way, the success of your work is directly related to the excellence of your *work* plan. The better your plan, the better your results will be.

There is an old saying that goes:

It's not that we plan to fail,
It's that we fail to plan!

Without a plan, the best that we can expect is to muddle through, hoping for some measure of success. But with a plan, our success is all mapped out for us.

A "plan" will do something amazing for you. It will literally allow you to work smarter instead of harder. I don't know about you, but I'll choose smarter any day of the week.

Designing A Work Plan

So, how *do* you plan your work? Is it complicated? Does it take a lot of time?

The answer to the last two questions is, "No". It isn't complicated and it doesn't take a lot of time. It's so simple a child could do it. In the following chapters I will show you how to build a *work plan* that will help you get all the work done that you need to do on a daily basis in order to keep your house neat and clean and operating efficiently and running smoothly. Whew! That's a mouth full! But true.

It's true because a *work plan* causes you to work with purpose, direction, and with very specific goals. It allows you to work smarter, not harder.

When you hear the work plan, you may think, "Why didn't I think of that?" Because, logically speaking, it makes perfect sense. It is a plan of action that is so easy to follow that you can use it every day of your life. Thus it is your Daily Routine.

This simple daily routine has only five little steps. And yet, don't underestimate it! You will be amazed at just how efficient this simple little routine really is.

OK, now, I have to come clean here. I don't want to mislead you. I've stated over and over again how *simple* this routine is. And that's true! But this particular routine is anything but sluggish! The truth be told, it is really quite zippy. It is energetic. It is snappy. In fact, I call it the *Snappy Daily Routine*. It will get your heart pumping and your muscles flexing. It will be a good supplement to your daily exercise routine.

What? You don't have one of those? Then let this be your first. It will probably be the only exercise routine you'll ever have that actually allows you to accomplish something tangible (besides toning your body, that is.)

Give it a try and see if it doesn't revolutionize your daily household work and get your heart a pumpin' to boot!

The Five-Step Snappy Daily Routine

*A*re you ready to get moving? Then here we go. This is it. The simple, snappy, five-step daily routine that helped save my sanity.

> *Note: Steps number 1, 2, and 4 of the Snappy Daily Routine apply to both the stay-at-home-mom and the mom who works outside her home. The mom who is employed outside her home may find it easier to modify steps three and five to fit her schedule.*

Step #1. Do the breakfast dishes

Every morning, as soon as you get up, you get dressed, and make your bed, right? Good for you! Then what do you do? If you are lake the vast majority, you eat breakfast. But what do you do after that? Well, there is almost no limit to the things you *could* do next. But I have a great suggestion. Why not *Do the breakfast dishes*? Do them ASAP.

Step #2. Plan tonight's dinner

With the breakfast dishes done, what should you do next? Well, since you are already in the kitchen, why not do one more kitchen-related thing before you move on. Now would be an excellent time to plan tonight's dinner. (Dream it up, write it down, check for ingredients, and remove any frozen ingredients from freezer and put in frig.)

Step #3 Start one load of laundry

OK, so far, so good. Nothing too challenging yet. But, hang on to your hats, we are about to pick up a little steam. Step number 3 of your Snappy Daily Routine is to start one load of laundry.

Note: If your family is large, you may have to do more than one load a day. A simple rule of thumb is one load of laundry per day for every two people. So, if there are four children in your household plus you and your husband, you could typically count on having to do three loads per day. Of course, that is just a rule of thumb. If your children are into sports or other activities that require several changes of clothes per day, that number could be higher. If your family is really neat and clean, they reuse their towels, and wear their clothes more than once, then that number could be lower. Whatever the case, step #3 is to start one load of laundry.

(Note: That load will be need to be transitioned from the washer to the dryer and from the dryer to being folded and put into closets and dressers at some point as you work your way through your Snappy Daily Routine.)

Step #4. Do your 5x5x5's (Said: Five-by-five-by-fives)

Note: A good kitchen timer is required for this step.

This is where the afterburners really kick in! While your washing machine is doing its thing, you can be tackling the next step of your daily routine. It is called the 5x5x5. This step requires a brisk, energetic, and aggressive level of activity (heart rate increasing level). Here's how it works:

> Set your timer for 5 minutes and quickly begin to do as much cleaning in one room of your house as you possibly can for that entire five minutes. Work briskly! Focus on that room and that room only. If it is already picked-up (as it should be) then you will have to go a little deeper to find something to do, such as dusting, vacuuming, cleaning mirrors and other glass surfaces, etc.
>
> Then, as soon as the timer goes off, scurry quickly to another room and clean *it* for five minutes. You will do this "five-minute-furry" of cleaning in five rooms of your house per day, five days of the week. Five rooms, five minutes, five days a week. Thus the name of this step: the 5x5x5. If you do the math, you will conclude that it takes 25 minutes. (Actually, you should figure on closer to 30 minutes because of the little bit of extra time it takes to transition between rooms.) So, the fourth step is to do your 5x5x5's.

Step #5. Bonus Room

Now we are down to the final step. It is called the Bonus Room. This is where you give one room of your house a little finer attention to the details. Every day, the Bonus Room will be a different room. One day you will give your kitchen a little bit more attention to the details, and another day you give your bathrooms that extra attention. Another day it could be your bedroom that receives a little deeper cleaning.

So, there you have a quick overview of the Snappy Daily Routine as it applies to the stay-at-home-mom. Now let's look at the Snappy Daily Routine for the mom who works outside her home.

For The Mom Who Works Outside Her Home

Starting one load of laundry before you leave for the day may not be the wisest thing to do, especially in hot weather. Therefore I recommend doing it after you get home. That way it can get moved through all the stages without hitting a delay somewhere along the line. And as for the Bonus Room step, how about coming up with a plan to equitably divide these "finer attention to details" chores among your family members, possibly being done on weekends. If not every weekend, then one or two a month. It sounds so reasonable that I'm sure your family will readily agree! After all, you have responsibilities outside the home just like they do, so why shouldn't everyone see the fairness of their pitching in and helping you at home? (OK, so I know they won't really be excited to help, but once you explain the justice of it all, they may go along even if they don't jump up and start dancing a little jig.)

The Art Of Delegation

I believe that every mom should have a firm grasp of the principle of delegation. And the mom who works outside her home should employ this principle to its fullest. Running a household is not a one-person job. And when you hold down another job besides the running of your household, you need all the help you can get. You are the manager of your home and as manager, there have to be people that you *manage*. The Five-Step Snappy Daily Routine is a great place to put your management skills to work...by delegating.

Remember: A good manager ALWAYS delegates.

But don't even dream of delegating before you have trained. Take the laundry, for example. You certainly wouldn't hand your child a basket-full of dirty clothes and just point him in the direction of your laundry room. Heaven only knows what you would get back. But if you train your children very carefully (starting around the age of 12), they can learn to do it very competently. (I know because I've done it—both trained my own children and been trained myself.) You begin by showing them every single stage

94

of doing a load of laundry from sorting by colors to folding and putting away. Then you work with them until you are confident they will not turn your whites pink, or your sweaters into Barbie Doll clothes, and then slowly relinquish control. Then, and this is a very important part, *assign* laundry detail to one of your newly trained recruits. (Caution: Don't leave any one person on any one particular duty too long. ROTATE CHORES!)

Another prime area where you can (and should) delegate is with your 5x5x5's! The way you do that is to is assign every member of the family a different room in which to diligently work for 5 minutes (their own bedrooms excluded). There could be five different rooms being worked on at the same time or just one room with five people working on it.

It's only 5 minutes for each person (if there are five members of your family), but what you end up with is 25 minutes worth of work. No doubt you will hear some fairly strenuous objections from your family when you make this request of them, but come on, even a busy teenaged jock with 3 dates per week, couldn't possibly deny you 5 minutes of his time each day…could he? This five-minute routine can even be done *before* work and school so as not to interfere with any after school activities.

I hate to keep beating a dead horse, but the value of the "family" labor pool is immeasurable to you. Get the help you need!

It is highly likely that the Bonus Room step will need to be done on weekends rather than throughout the week, even with the help of family.

But there is one other option. Why not consider hiring help for some of the deeper cleaning. Once a month you could have someone come in and help you catch up with the finer details. Even 2 or 3 hours a month would help immensely. (If you can work it into your budget, that is.)

As a Mom with an outside career and the manager of your home, you need to fully enlist the help of every family member. You should make delegation your new best friend.

In review, the five steps of the Snappy Daily Routine are:

#1.   **Do Breakfast Dishes**

#2.   **Plan Tonight's Dinner**

#3.   **Start One Load of Laundry**

#4.   **Do your 5x5x5's**

- **Move laundry load to dryer**
- **Start another load if necessary**

#5.   **Bonus Room**

A Closer Look

I realize that this is a very quick mention of the five steps of the Snappy Daily Routine. These points really deserve a closer look, but I didn't want to have one chapter that went on and on and on by explaining each of these steps in a single chapter. So I decided to make a separate chapter for each step. That way, if you have precious little time for reading (in other words, if you are a mom) then you are lucky indeed if you can grab your book and get one small chapter read before someone knocks on your bathroom door. And getting a chance to read a really, really long chapter, well, you might as well forget it. Therefore, I have chosen to explain each of the five steps of the Snappy Daily Routine in five separate chapters.

So, grab your book, sit down, put your feet up (unless you are in the bathroom), and hope for a few quiet moments to get through a chapter.

CHAPTER 12

Step #1 of Your Snappy Daily Routine

Step #1– Do the breakfast dishes.

Riddle: Why are dishes are like rabbits?
Answer: Because they multiply quickly!

Have you ever noticed that if you leave a few dirty dishes in the sink, by the time you come back later to do them, they have multiplied? Why do you suppose this happens? It is because those few dishes you left behind acted as an attractant to any other dirty dishes that happened to come along later. No one knows for sure exactly *how* this phenomenon happens (because no one has ever actually witnessed it) but I have my own theory. On those busy days in your household when your family eats in shifts, I believe that your husband or your children come along a little after you, carrying their own dirty dishes to the kitchen. They came, fully intending to rinse off their dishes and put them in the dishwasher, when they suddenly noticed that there were already dirty dishes in the sink. What a stroke of luck! Taking a quick glance around to be sure no one is watching they hurriedly place their own dishes in on top of yours and quickly scurry away from the scene of the crime. By the time you come back to clean up the *small* mess you left behind earlier, it has grown into a *huge* mess! And you can't even scold anyone because you set the precedence yourself!

Consequently, the first step of your Snappy Daily Routine is to do the breakfast dishes *immediately* following breakfast.

By the way, this also applies to each and every meal of the day. Never, ever leave dishes to be done at a later time. Back in my pre-organized days I used to "leave dishes to be done later" on a regular basis. Often, I would get up in the morning only to be greeted by last night's dirty dinner dishes. It was enough to turn your stomach (especially when pregnant)! But I always had a good excuse for not doing the dishes right after a meal. I was always too tired from working so hard to make the meal in the first place, too full from eating the meal, or too overwhelmed by all the other disorganization in my life. Whichever excuse I happened to be using at the time, it always seemed appropriate and justified. It was easy to convince myself that I actually *deserved* not to have to do them right at that point in time.

Ah, but I always regretted that decision later. Immediate gratification produces delayed irritation.

The Solution

There is no magic wand that you can wave to eliminate dishes all together. But there is something you can do to cut back on the amount of work that has to be done immediately following a meal. And that is to "clean as you go" while preparing the meal, so that by the time the meal is on the table, much of the work is already done.

I have a challenge for you. Immediately following a big meal, take a good look around at the dishes that have to be done. Are there pots and pans and utensils from the preparation process? If so, then you are stockpiling! Once I began to get organized, one of the steps I took to gain control of my life was to stop *stockpiling* dirty dishes. I began using the "clean as you go" method instead. I made it my goal to get most, if not all, of the preparation dishes (pots, pans, measuring cups and utensils) done before we sat down to eat.

And in a perfect world, I would get all of them done all of the time. But ours is not a perfect world. So, even on those occasions when I can only get some of the prep dishes done, I still enjoy my meal more knowing there are fewer dishes to deal with when my tummy is full, my energy is sluggish, and my will to get things done is zapped.

> *Note: Obviously, this will mean that the meal will be a little slower getting to the table. So don't call your family to eat until YOU are ready. Otherwise, they may get a little restless. Better yet, get some of that family of yours in the kitchen to help you with all this work.*

Then, following the meal, all you have to do is the dishes used for eating and whatever prep dishes you weren't able to finish! It makes a tremendous difference in the post-meal clean up to be done.

But wait, there's more!

There is particular mealtime rule that we, as a family, adopted many years ago. It is such a wonderful and beneficial rule that I believe EVERY family should adopt it and have it carved in stone! It should be firm, non-negotiable, and strictly enforced! It should be so ingrained, so instilled, and so drilled into each person that they would feel like they were leaving the table naked if they didn't abide by it. And that is the "Everyone is Responsible" rule. Which means that each member of the family is responsible for his or her own place setting at the table. After the meal each person is to carry his or her own plate, drinking glass, and silverware to the sink, and to throw their napkin into the trash—instead of leaving everything on the table for the maid or slave (a.k.a. mom) to take care of.

Note: I remember one episode of the Brady Bunch where the whole family (mom, dad, and all six kids included) finished a meal and then simply got up from the table and walked away. They left every single item behind for poor Alice to take care of. Inconceivable! It made me hoppin' mad! I know that it was only a TV show and that Alice didn't really have to carry all those dishes to the sink all by herself, but I thought it sent a terrible message. "You can be as irresponsible as you wish, and as lazy as you want, because someone else will clean up after you!" In our case, I knew that someone else wouldn't be Alice, it would be ME!

I guess instead of being mad at the writers of The Brady Bunch, I should be thankful to them because I've been able to use the family's behavior in that episode as a prime example of what NOT TO DO!

Then, if you wish, you can even carry the Everyone is Responsible Rule one step further and require each person to rinse his or her own dishes and load them into the dishwasher. It's all about *responsibility!* Learning it, teaching it, and living it.

Speaking of responsibility, one day Tom and I learned a very valuable lesson in responsibility from a most unusual source...a 2½ year-old.

We were visiting at the home of some friends when we witnessed something that had a profound and lasting impact on us. Tom and I were sitting at the family's kitchen table visiting with the mom of the family who was busy tossing a salad that she was making. The father had made a quick trip to the corner store for some last-minute item and was just returning. When he walked in the front door he spotted their 2½ year-old son in the living room busily unloading a bookshelf, systematically taking every book and happily tossing it to the floor. The dad stopped in his tracks, looked directly at his son and asked sternly, "Grant! Who is responsible for you?"

Now, Tom and I, being the astute parents that we were, quickly turned our gaze to the mother, whom we deemed to be in a bit of trouble right now with the dad for allowing their little angel to make such a mess. To our astonishment, "mom" kept right on tossing her salad without missing a beat.

So, our heads immediately swung back to the center of the controversy... the child. At that time, the little fellow looked up at his father and answered quietly, "me." "That's right!" his daddy confirmed emphatically. "YOU are responsible for YOU! So what are YOU going to do about this mess that you've made?" "Clean...up," came the response. "Right!" said the father. "Clean it up, right away!"

Which... he did. It took him considerably longer to load the shelves than it did to unload, but he kept at it until every book was off the floor and onto a shelf. Of course, the job looked like a 2½-year-old had done it, but it got done.

WOW! We were blown away. If this child, at such a tender age, could be taught such a valuable life lesson then why couldn't everyone be taught? If parents everywhere would teach their children that *they* are the ones who are responsible for their own actions, and if we ourselves would take full responsibility for *our* own actions, just imagine what a different world this would be.

These days you hear people all the time clamoring about their rights. It's my "right" to do this. It's my "right" to do that. But oddly enough, you don't hear these same people say, it's my "responsibility" to do this or my "responsibility" to do that.

And yet, with every *right* comes a *responsibility*. It is our *right* as husband and wife to have children and with that *right* come many *responsibilities*. Ironically enough, one of those *responsibilities* is to teach *responsibility* to our children.

———

Now, getting back to the original topic of this chapter…the dishes. It is our *right* to eat, but with that *right* comes the *responsibility* of doing the dishes. Not when we "feel" like it. Not when it is convenient. Not when all of the other dishes in the cupboard are dirty so that there are no clean dishes left to use unless we wash some…but immediately following our meal (or snack)! That is the responsible thing to do.

If it is hard to do the dishes immediately, that's OK. Go ahead and do them right away anyway. Don't give in to the temptation of waiting. You will be happier later that you didn't wait…because, believe me, it only gets harder as time passes! Not to mention the fact that those dishes, like rabbits, multiply.

This next section I am dedicating to all of those who may not have had a hardened Drill Sargent for a mom like I did. As I mentioned before, my mom diligently taught me many household skills. Included in those skills was how to do the dishes, I mean, how to *really* do the dishes. Believe it or not, washing the actual dirty plates, glasses, and silverware is not all that there is to "doing the dishes".

> *Note: I love my husband. In fact, Tom is so perfect for me that I'm sure God must have made him just for me. That being said (so that no one could possibly think that I am complaining about or unhappy with this man of my dreams), I will say this about him. He has no clue how to "follow through" with doing the dishes. Of course, he is always willing to step in and give it the old college try, but oh, my goodness. The things he leaves "undone" are enough*

to boggle the mind! To him, doing the dishes means washing the actual dishes that happened to have gotten dirty during the process of eating the meal. Nothing more—nothing less. But because my mom taught me how to do the dishes from the time I was knee high to the kitchen sink, I know that there is much, much more to it than that. Thanks to my mom, I how to "follow-through" when doing the dishes. So, to all the wonderful wives, moms, and homemakers out there who may have been deprived of this vital slice of education, allow me to be your drill instructor for just a bit. This is...

How To "Follow-through" When Doing The Dishes

- Clean as you go while cooking and preparing the meal
    (As soon as you are done with a utensil, pot, pan, measuring cup, etc., wash it and put it away or put it in the dishwasher.)
- After the meal—completely clear the table
    (Don't leave *anything* behind that doesn't belong on the table—even something as small and insignificant as a rumpled napkin gives the whole table a messy look.)
- Properly store all leftovers
    (If there is just a small amount of something left, put it into a smaller dish and cover tightly before putting it in the refrigerator.)
- Scrape all food scraps from plates into the trash or disposal
- Rinse all dishes and put them into dishwasher (or wash by hand if you don't have a dishwasher)
- Wash the table—and dry if necessary
- Shake off crumbs from place mats

(Avoid the temptation of shaking crumbs onto the floor. I know it is easier than walking across the floor with the place mats to the sink or trash and shaking them there, but *really!* You don't dump the last of the milk from a glass onto the floor, do you? So, why shake the crumbs there?)

- Put place mats back on the table neatly
- Replace center piece
- Push chairs up tightly to the table
- Wipe down all countertops
- Don't leave odds and ends out on your countertops.

(Sometimes, after all the dishes are done, there might be a few items that you just don't know what to do with. *Make a decision!* Do *something* with those items. But whatever you do, don't leave them out on the counter top or shoved into a corner somewhere. These items immediately catch the eye of everyone who enters the kitchen. For a crisp, clean, look—find a proper place for those odds and ends items.)

- Wipe off the top of your stove to remove any grease or food splatters
- Thoroughly rinse and wring out your rag (or sponge)

(Never leave them sitting in a soggy heap in the bottom of your sink! Not only do they look yucky there, but they become a breeding ground for bacteria. Wring out your rag thoroughly and hang it up to dry. Squeeze sponges dry and put them where air can circulate around them. You can get ceramic sponge holders designed specifically for holding kitchen sponges. And—be sure to launder your rags often! There is nothing worse than a smelly dishrag! I like to buy rags that are mostly white so that I can bleach them. Nothing cuts the smell or kills the germs like good old bleach!)

- Give your kitchen floor a quick sweep—especially around and under the high chair if you have a baby
- Think you're done? Well, you're getting close, but not quite.

There's one minor detail I forgot to mention. You know those little drain baskets in the bottom of your sink? Well, they are there for a reason—to catch food scraps and keep them from clogging your drain. You absolutely MUST empty them into the trash! Otherwise the scraps just sit there rotting, looking ugly, and restricting the water from draining properly.

(Note: I was teaching a home organization class years ago and when I mentioned this point one lady told the class that when she was growing up her mother made her eat any food scraps that she failed to empty from the drain baskets! Oh, gag! Now, that's what I call child abuse! I'll admit, emptying the drain basket is important, but nothing is that important. I only mentioned this story so that it would create such a vivid picture in your mind that it would serve to jog your memory, reminding you to empty your own drain baskets.)

OK, so now you're done! Now that you know all of the steps for "following through" when doing the dishes, what do you think? Is it too overwhelming? Are you never eating again or feeding your family again? Or are you eating *out* from now on?

Well, believe me, I know that there are a lot of steps to following through with the dishes, but they are not MAJOR steps, there are just LOTS of them. Once you get used to them, they will seem as natural as brushing your teeth before bed.

One mother complained bitterly when I told her that she should always attempt to do the dishes *immediately* after the meal. She said the mere thought gave her a headache. However, she also said she would try it. "But", she added, "it won't be any fun".

My question to her was, "Will it be any *more* fun later?"

CHAPTER 13

Step #2 of Your
Snappy Daily Routine

Step #2—PLAN TONIGHT'S DINNER

*I*n this day and age of junk food, fast food restaurants, and ready-made-meals, does anyone actually cook dinner any more? Well, I certainly hope so. And, if I have to, I will go on a one-woman-crusade to see that this age-old tradition doesn't die.

Just imagine a feast of mashed potatoes (made from real potatoes), gravy, tender juicy meat, vegetables, a salad (either mixed greens or Jell-O with fruit), fresh rolls with creamy butter melting on top, and a side dish of pickles and olives or radishes and green onions. Then top it all off with a slice of pie or cake with a scoop of ice cream on top. It's more than a meal…it's tradition. It's family. It's togetherness. It's worth it!

If you like the sounds of this as much as I do, then NOW (immediately after doing the breakfast dishes) is the time to decide what to serve for dinner tonight, not at 5 o'clock tonight!

In my pre-organized days I often suffered from an ailment that I call "brain freeze" (not to be confused with the sudden, severe pain in your head from eating ice cream too quickly). When it came time to make dinner, my brain would freeze up. All I could ever think of was the same three meals. So we had those three meals over and over again. Once in a while I would break away from that rut and make something different. Even when my family cheered from delight at the sight and taste of something new, it didn't dawn on me to include that dish in my menu selection. Oh, my! I was a hopeless scatterbrain. So, we had the same three dinners over and over again.

Early planning is the key to a wider variety in your menu selections.

> *Note: Now, you may be wondering, "Won't it be just as hard to think of a dinner plan early in the day as it would be just prior to dinner?" The answer is, no, not at all. Because there is not the stress of a ticking clock reminding you that you are running out of time.*

After making your selection, be sure to remove anything from the freezer that needs time to defrost and put it in the refrigerator. Also, if you decide on a salad, Jell-O dish, or something else that can be prepared in advance, go ahead and make it now, put it in the refrigerator and then at dinnertime, presto! Just pull it out and put it on the table. No fuss, no muss. This is a wonderful thing you can do for yourself that will save you time later, not to mention last-minute frustrations as you're trying to put a meal together.

> *Note: For some of you, this will be hard to believe. But there was once a time "before" microwave ovens. I know, because I was alive in those pre-historic days. Back then, if you didn't remember to remove something from the freezer early enough in the day, you were stuck with trying to defrost it under hot water. It was hard, slow, and painstaking. But today we have the wonderful advantage of the microwave oven. Ahh! If you forget to defrost early, you can always use the speed and convenience of the microwave.*

Another advantage to early planning is that you can avoid the unpleasant surprise of discovering, at the last minute, that you lack one of the key ingredients in a dish you are preparing. (Been there, done that!) I once got right down to the rolling out of my dough for cinnamon rolls when I discovered that I didn't have any cinnamon. (Somehow, they just weren't the same without it.) By planning early, you can either go buy what you need or choose to make something different.

No frantic straining-of-the-brain to figure out what to make. No last minute dashes to the corner store to pick up a missing ingredient. You will feel so "in control".

The Food-idea Book

One day my friend Mary told me how to make a food IDEA book. It turned out to be the greatest thing since sliced bread and the sure cure for brain-freeze! Here's how it works. Take a three-ring-binder, put divider pages in it (the kind with tabs on the sides) and put a couple of sheets of notebook paper behind each divider page.

Next, label each tab with a different food category:

MEATS

VEGETABLES

BREADS

SANDWICHES

CASSEROLES

SOUPS

SALADS

DESSERTS

SNACKS

Now comes the fun part. Every time you think of a particular food that you know your family likes in one of the categories, write it on one of the sheets of paper under the proper heading. Don't strain your brain by trying to fill out the whole book at one sitting. You may think you could never make such a book, because, after all, your brain freezes up when you try to think of food ideas. But you will be surprised just how often a food idea will pop into your mind when you're *not* trying to think of something to cook. When it does, hurry to your book and write it down before it gets away. When you want to really concentrate on adding items to your book, sit down with a few cookbooks, magazines and your recipe file. Go through them to get ideas.

Note: You are not making a "cookbook" so don't include recipes. Instead, next to the food idea, write down where the recipe can be found. If it is in a cookbook or magazine be sure to record the page number as well as the name of the book or magazine.

It took me several weeks to make my Food Idea Book. In fact, it is the kind of thing that might never actually be completed because, from time to time, I still run across a new item that I decide to add to it. It is a work in progress. But I was able to compile the bulk of ideas in just a few weeks time. Now, when I try a new recipe and find that we really like it or when I see a dish being prepared on the cooking channel that makes me salivate just looking at it, I quickly add it to the proper category of my book.

My Food Idea Book is one of my all time favorite books. It is literally filled with idea, after idea, after idea. Even now, it is still fun to sit down with it and go through the well-worn pages. Everything in it is something yummy and wonderful (because I didn't write anything in it that wasn't). It makes for fascinating reading. (I guess you can tell that I really enjoy food.) My Food Idea Book is as captivating to me as a good novel. I just love it.

So, immediately after finishing the breakfast dishes, I sit down with a cup of coffee and flip through its pages until I find a main dish that sounds too good to resist. Then I look through the pages of the other categories (salads, vegetables, breads, desserts, etc) and make my choices to round out my meal plan. Next, I check to be sure that I have all the necessary ingredients for making each of the dishes. Any part of that meal that can be made ahead of time, I go ahead and prepare right then.

Mealtimes are much less stressful since I started planning them in advance. They are less boring, more nutritious, more interesting, more delicious and, yes, even more *fun!*

CHAPTER 14

Step #3 of Your
Snappy Daily Routine

Step #3—START A LOAD OF LAUNDRY

*T*his step is certainly one that could be considered "optional" because some people might prefer doing all of their laundry in one day rather than one or two loads per day. I don't enjoy doing laundry very much. It's one of my very weakest points. So for me, personally, I would rather do a little at a time than to devote a good portion of any given day to it.

But in my pre-organized days, I did not do my laundry the way I now do it (a little at a time). In fact, I disliked doing the laundry so much that I simply ignored it. I put it off until my poor family had nothing left to wear. When I look back on it now, I am simply appalled at my method of choice for doing the laundry.

In those days, we didn't own a clothes hamper. Our laundry room *was* our clothes hamper. Every member of the family would simply give their dirty clothes a heave into the laundry room, letting them fall to the floor. Then, once the door could no longer be opened without the aid of two strong men and a boy, I knew it was time to tackle the laundry.

I would start my laundry day early and work until late into the night. My routine went something like this:

- Sort the enormous pile of clothes by colors
- Stuff the first load into the washing machine
- Put the washed load of clothes into the dryer
- Re-start the washing machine with the next load
- As soon as the first load was dry, put it into a laundry basket
- Carry that basket upstairs to our bedroom
- Empty the basket onto our bed and carry the empty basket back to the laundry room
- Repeat this process (over and over and over again) until all the loads were finished or until it was bedtime (whichever came first)

In the meantime, while the washing machine was sloshing back and forth and the dryer was tumbling round and round, I would scurry around the house trying to get other things accomplished. By bedtime I would be exhausted and our bed would be piled high with clean, unfolded, badly rumpled clothes. I would then begin the tremendous task of trying to get that virtual mountain of clean clothes folded *before* I collapsed from exhaustion.

Often, the mountain won. When I couldn't take it any more, I would end up shoving the remainder of the pile off onto the floor in order to have a spot on the bed to collapse my weary body. Then, first thing the next morning, I would have to face that jumbled mess of clean clothes lying on the floor. Trust me, it's not a good way to start your day!

Yikes! It's hard to believe that that was the way I *chose* to do the laundry. Not only did my poor family have nothing left to wear by laundry day, but I also created a whole lot of unnecessary work for myself. Most clothing articles, if immediately removed from the dryer and folded or hung on a hanger, did not require any ironing. But the way I did it, even the permanent press had to be ironed! Sometimes I even had to re-wash entire loads after I had pushed them off the bed, because they got mixed up with the dirty clothes still lying on the floor. (Yet another little indicator of just how undisciplined we were). Obviously, something had to change.

The Solution

Since I didn't think my family would agree to quit wearing clothes, I came to the conclusion that *I* was the one who would have to make the change. Once I made the firm resolution to solve my laundry day woes, I started by literally *forcing* myself to stand at the dryer and removing the clean clothes one article at a time. I never, never, never again allowed myself to put a load of clean, unfolded, clothes into a laundry basket. You talk about a hard thing to do! I am a flighty person. I would rather do a little bit of work over here and then run over there and do a little bit more work, then run somewhere else and do a little more over there…than to completely finish any one project before moving on the next. So to stand at the dryer, feet firmly planted, until every single item had been taken care of was almost physically painful for me. Nevertheless, I forced myself to do it. Time and time again I would catch myself trying to make a break for the door half or three-quarters of the way through the job and would literally have to drag myself back to finish the task.

Then, and this is equally important, as soon as I was finished emptying the dryer, I put *everything* away. I didn't allow myself the luxury of leaving all of those neat little piles of clean, folded clothes lying about. I immediately loaded the piles into a basket and delivered them to the proper rooms and put them into their respective drawers. I also took all the clothes that were on hangers and put them into the closets where they belonged.

By the end of my first "laundry day" under this new system, I knew I was on to something. I didn't have that mountain of clean clothes on my bed to have to deal with at bedtime. And (yippee!) the "no-iron" clothes stayed that way! I was delighted beyond belief and felt a tremendous sense of satisfaction. But it was still a long, hard, labor-intensive day. (When you have ten to fifteen loads to do, just by nature of the fact that it takes a certain amount of time for the washer and dryer to do their thing, it ends up taking all day long to process that many loads.)

So, I decided to try a radical new approach. Instead of cramming all of the laundry into one day, I decided to experiment with distributing that huge one-day job over the period of several days. After all, it did seem logical that it would be easier to do a *little* laundry every day than a whole *lot* of laundry all on the same day. Since I had just finished all of the laundry the day before and our hamper (a.k.a. our laundry room) was empty, it seemed like the perfect time to start a new system.

It also seemed like the perfect time to buy an actual hamper. I wouldn't need anything nearly as large as the one we had been using since our laundry would no longer be piling up for days and weeks on end. Someone had recently told me about a system for storing the dirty laundry by colors. They called it the "3-Basket Method". It was an ingenious system that sounded like a little slice of heaven to me. So I made provisions to implement it immediately.

I bought three identical laundry baskets and set them on the floor of the laundry room along one wall. I labeled each one with the color of clothes that it was to hold and then called for a family meeting right there in the laundry room. I informed my husband and two children that, as a family, we were no longer going to be using the laundry room floor as our clothes hamper. These three new baskets were going to take its place. For a few moments they stared at me like I was speaking a foreign language. And, just to confound them even more, I proceeded to tell them that they each had to *sort* their own laundry as they deposited it into the baskets. (The look of utter disbelief on their faces was priceless!) But I didn't stop there. I also explained that I wanted them to check through their pockets first—*before* putting their clothes into the baskets. I ventured further, "If I happen to find anything of value in your pockets later as I'm putting clothes into the washer, I might mistake it for a tip that you are trying to leave me as a token of your appreciation for all the hard work I do." (The look on their faces turned from disbelief to amusement. They thought I was kidding! But I glared at them in a stone cold manner, which they knew meant I was dead serious.) I wasn't the most popular woman on the planet that day, but it was a price I was willing to pay.

Well, they all got used to the idea fairly quickly. I had to be patient with them at first though, because they often made mistakes in sorting. I was always careful to glance through every load as I was putting it into the washing machine, especially the white load. If a red article happened to accidentally end up with the white clothes, everything in that load would be turned pink (including Tom's underwear!). I have to praise my bright family because they actually caught on amazingly quickly. As time went by they made fewer and fewer mistakes. Once we all got into the routine of it, the system proved to be almost miraculous. I give it a great big A+!

Note: Thank goodness, someone got smart and came up with a segmented hamper that allows you to sort your clothes by color as you put them into it. I have one and wouldn't be without it! It takes up much less space than the three laundry baskets.

Another note: It is absolutely imperative that you check pockets as you unload a basket into the washing machine. I'm sure we've all experienced washing a tissue. As exasperating as that can be, it doesn't compare to washing a color crayon. Actually, it isn't the washing that is so bad, but the drying! The crayon melts, spreads, and irreversibly speckles everything in the load. And how many of us have washed our husbands' wallets? I certainly have! I've done more money laundering in my day than most drug dealers! It doesn't do the leather wallet any good either. So, my advice—check all pockets of all clothes before you wash them. This applies even if you've been diligent to train your family to clean out their pockets before putting their clothes into the hamper. Goodness knows—I've even found things in my own pockets at the last minute!

While the washing machine is running, go on to the next step of your routine. *As soon as the washer is finished,* transfer that load to the dryer and put another load into the washer (if you are doing more than one load for that day).

Likewise, *just as soon as the dryer is finished running* (set the buzzer to alert you), take care of that load immediately, by either folding the items or hanging them on hangers. Then put those clothes away—all of them! I know some moms who choose to have each member their family put their own stacks of clothes away as part of their daily routine. And that is certainly fine, as long as you follow through and make sure that they actually DO IT!

Personally, I love doing my laundry this way. It beats my old way all to pieces. Instead of having this looming responsibility hanging over my head, instead of having my family murmuring about having nothing left to wear, and instead of having an unsightly heap of dirty clothes piling higher and higher, I now have incredible victory in this area of my life. My laundry is caught up, my laundry room is neat, and our closets and dresser drawers are full of sweet smelling, neatly folded clothes. And every member of my family (including myself) has something to smile about.

CHAPTER 15

Step #4 of Your
Snappy Daily Routine

Step #4—Do your 5x5x5's (said: five-by-five-by-fives).

*O*K, so what is a 5x5x5, anyway? What do all of those 5's stand for? Well, it's very simple. They stand for:

5 Rooms

5 Minutes

5 Days a Week

Here's how it works. Choose 5 target rooms each day and spend 5 minutes in each of those rooms cleaning like mad. Repeat this procedure 5 days a week. If you have more than 5 rooms in your house you will have to rotate rooms in order to incorporate all of the rooms of your home on a regular basis. Some rooms of your house may not be used as heavily or frequently as others are (like a guest bedroom). In such a case, that room may only need to be to be cleaned once a month or when a guest is coming, so don't put it into the regular rotation. Other rooms, such as your living room and kitchen, get used a lot so they will need to be included in the rotation every day.

This is not meant to be a deep cleaning, rather a super spiffer-upper. The idea is to spend 5 minutes in each room working at a brisk pace. At the end of only 25 minutes, you will see surprising results in those 5 rooms.

What You Will Need:

1. A good kitchen timer
2. Cleaning Supplies
3. Carrying Case for Cleaning Supplies
4. Super Burst of Energy!!

The Timer

Most of you are too young to remember a TV show many, many years ago called Beat the Clock. Contestants were given the challenge of completing a certain task before the time on the clock ran out. If they beat the clock, they won a prize. In the 5x5x5 you are also given the challenge of beating the clock, or in this case, the timer. So, to play this little game, you will first need a timer. I have a small digital one that I use. It works perfectly for this application because I can glance at it from time to time and know exactly how much longer I have left. I set my timer for 5 minutes before I begin working in each room. Then I push the start button and race around as quickly as possible to accomplish the absolute most that I can in that 5 minutes. It's like a contest—it's me against the timer. When the timer rings, I stop working (of course, sometimes when the timer goes off, it catches me mid-way through a little project that I don't want to leave dangling, so I finish it rather than leaving it half done). Then I quickly move to the next room and push the start button again and zip through that room. Since we rarely leave anything out of place any more, I get the privilege of doing other things besides just picking up items that are strewn around the house. (What an incredible benefit that has turned out to be!)

Cleaning Supplies And Carry Case

As I go from room to room, I am armed with my dust rag, can of furniture polish, window cleaner, cleanser, disinfecting wipes, etc. I carry all these cleaning supplies in a plastic carrying-tote with a handle on top. This tote moves with me from room to room so that all of the supplies I need are at my fingertips and I don't have to run back and forth to another room to get what I need. If I had to use valuable seconds running back and forth, it would greatly decrease my productivity. This way, every second counts!

Burst Of Energy

If you don't already have an exercise program, the 5x5x5 will provide you with a little burst of activity that can actually make you sweat if you move at the recommended pace. Recommended pace: Brisk!

As in any competition (remember, you're racing against the timer) you want to give it all you've got. So, work carefully, but work like you're out to win something. And in a way, you are! You're working to win the battle against clutter, chaos, and disorder. Your prize? Freedom, joy, and an ever increasing sense of satisfaction.

What You Can Expect

When you first begin to practice the 5x5x5 step of your daily routine, you may look at a particular room and think, "What good will 5 minutes do in this room that is so out-of-control?" Let me assure you, you will be amazed at how much good it will do! Because today you will do 5 minutes in that room, tomorrow you will do 5 more minutes, and the next day 5 more. By the end of the week you will have spent 25 minutes in that room. If you are practicing the responsibility rule yourself and if you are training your family not to sabotage your accomplishments, you will soon be looking at that same room and thinking, "What can I possibly spend 5 minutes doing in a room that looks this perfect?"

25 Minutes A Day

It may not be rocket science. It may be so simple that it seems pointless. But sometimes, the simplest things in life are the most profound. When facing an overwhelming obstacle, we may wonder what good a mere twenty-five minutes could possibly do?

The answer is: WORLDS AND WORLDS OF GOOD! The consistent, persistent chipping away at that obstacle will eventually cause it to crumble.

Look at the Grand Canyon. If you had told that little river that runs through it, "I want you to go over there and cut a huge, deep canyon through those rocks." It might have said, "No way! That is a ridiculous notion. It is completely impossible!"

Well, yeah! I should think! Especially if you told that river to do it all in one fell swoop. But the river took it a little bit at a time, hardly noticing the effort *or* the results until it looked back later. I'm sure that when it did look back and it thought, "Wow! Did *I* do that? I never thought I had it in me. Well, my, my, my. If I do say so myself, I am amazed!"

No matter how huge your obstacle is, if you will chip away at it a little at a time, you will fashion and form your own "Grand Canyon". And you will be down right amazed with yourself when you look back at what you were able to accomplish with just 25 little minutes a day.

Step #5 of Your Snappy Daily Routine

Step #5—Bonus Room

*T*his is it...the last step of the *Snappy Daily Routine* that literally rescued me from a world of confusion and disorder. This five-step routine revolutionized my work habits by giving me the direction I needed. It gave me a much-needed plan to follow for getting my work done. It was such a perfectly balanced and well-thought out plan that it transformed *everything* in my life, not just my work and the condition of my house, but everything. Before, my entire life revolved around the work I needed to do, the fact that I could never get it all done (no matter how hard I tried), and around the constant feeling of guilt that followed me like a dark cloud.

But *now*, with this awesome plan to follow, everything is different. I'm liberated at last! Yes, it was through the use of a structured plan. Yes, it has very specific steps to be followed at very specific times. Yes, it looks like a form of "control". *But consider this…*

There was a revolution in the 1960's. It was a breaking away from the rules and regulations that, according to a segment of society, had kept the human race in bondage for the beginning of time. But now, thanks to this uprising, these people were free at last! Free to do whatever they wanted. Free to be wild. Free to throw out the rules. Free to disobey authority. Free to do drugs until their brains blew up. Free to do whatever felt good.

But...were they really free? Were their lives better as a result? Or, did everything go a little "haywire" because suddenly, there was no order in their lives, there were no boundaries to protect them, and there were no directions for them to follow.

Interestingly enough, the opposite of order is—chaos.
The opposite of having boundaries is—
being out of control.
The opposite of having directions to follow is—
being disoriented or lost.

Well, in my own breaking away from the rules after I got married, I managed to pretty well mess up my life. I was lost, disoriented, out of control, and living in complete chaos. No, I never did drugs or any of that really wild stuff, but in my own way, I rebelled just the same. I didn't want anyone else ruling my life, telling me what to do or, for that matter, even making suggestions. But when my life crashed and burned at the bottom of the cliff, when I got good and miserable enough...I became desperate for the rules, the order, the boundaries, and some good reliable directions to follow. (Have you ever been lost in the woods? You'd give anything for a map!) Well, that was just how desperate I felt. And that's just how welcomed the "map" was that guided me to freedom.

I said all of that because the *Snappy Daily Routine* may seem like such a structured plan that it doesn't appeal to you, especially if you are a free-spirited kind of person. And this final step in particular may seem like something you could easily live without. And, in all honesty, I guess you could. But this step is the one that crowns all the rest. It's the one that separates the *average* from the *excellent*. Not everyone does this step. And certainly, YOU don't have to. But if you choose to do it your house will take a hyper-leap in appearance.

This step is the equivalent to the "follow-through" portion of doing the dishes. It is the "finer attention to details" that many people are clueless about. For example, some people may not even be aware that the build-up of gunk around the base of their kitchen faucet is a condition that doesn't have to happen. (They may not know that that is what toothbrushes were made for. Well, if not as their primary function, definitely as their secondary.)

This fifth step is an indispensable part of making your home look and feel the very best that it can. Like I said before, it is the crowning touch to all the others.

How It Works

Five days a week, you will choose a different room of your house to devote a little bit of extra attention to. This is the *Bonus Room* for the day, kind of like employee-of-the-month or student-of-the-week.

For the sake of example, I will share my own choices with you. Years ago, I decided that I wanted Mondays to be the day that I devote extra attention to my kitchen. So that is the way it has been all of these years. And to this day, the word *Monday* is synonymous with *kitchen* to me. I love starting my week with my kitchen in tip-top condition. My weekly Bonus Room schedule goes like this:

Monday	—	Kitchen
Tuesday	—	Living Room
Wednesday	—	Bathrooms
Thursday	—	Rotation Room *(*See note on next page)*
Friday	—	Bedrooms

(*Note: This is the day of the week that I rotate the rooms that I devote extra attention to. These are the rooms that don't necessarily need the finer attention to details every single week. So on this day, I alternately put them into the rotation. They are rooms such as the office/den, laundry room, family room, etc.)

The Finer Attention To Details

What on earth does the "finer attention" mean, anyway? Well, it means to look a little deeper, to see the things that you may not notice at first glance, and then to take care of them. Now, I suppose that most of us, eventually, do take care of these details. But by doing them frequently they remain "minor details" instead of becoming "major details".

The Details

Now, just what are those delightful little "details", anyway? Well, I will go room by room, step by step, in an attempt to *detail* the details.

Below is a close-up look at the finer little details that need to be done in each room. I am not saying that every single detail has to be done every single week. Of course, if you have the time and your circumstances allow, then that would be wonderful. But some mothers of young children or those with other demanding circumstances may only be able to do one or two of these details per room, per day. Do as much as you can, and what you can't get done this week, do another week.

Kitchen

- **Scour the kitchen sink**

  Be sure to include the sink stopper. Turn it over and give the whole thing a good rubdown with your cleanser and rag.

- **Thoroughly wash countertops**

  Pull out any appliances or nick-nacks and clean in behind them.

- **Polish all appliances**

  Refrigerator—front, top, sides, handles

  Range—top, front, knobs, drip pans

  Toaster—empty crumbs from tray underneath

  Microwave—inside and out

  (Hint: Put a large bowl of hot water in your microwave, set "cook-time" for five minutes, and let it run. Then let the bowl of steaming water set in the enclosed space for several minutes. Then take it out and wipe down the inside. This does an amazing job of softening and loosening food splatters.)

- **Sweep and mop floor**

  Shake throw rugs and sweep under them

  (One lady once told us that her cat got stuck to her kitchen floor. I think she waited just a little too long to mop!)

- **Wipe off windowsill**

- **Clean and dust decorations and nick-nacks**

Living Room

- **Remove cobwebs**

- **Dust**

- **Vacuum**

  (Don't hesitate to get out the hose portion of your vacuum and get in and around furniture, along baseboards, and under furniture cushions— especially if you allow eating your living room.)

- **Clean all hard surfaces**

  Mirrors

  Table Tops

  Lamps

  TV Screen

  Candle holders and all other Decorations

Bathrooms

- Sweep down cobwebs

- Scour sink and tub

  (With soft-scrub cleanser and an old toothbrush, scrub around the base of your faucet, the chrome ring around the drain openings, and around the faucet handles. Then polish dry with a soft cloth.)

- Clean mirror

  (I have found that plain old water works amazingly well as a cleaning agent. And, it doesn't leave streaks like some glass cleaners can. Pretty cheat, too! Use a soft cloth—like a section of an old receiving blanket—to polish it dry.)

- Clean toilet

  (Hint: If you have young boys, you may want to do this more often than weekly—like maybe, daily. Especially if they are just learning to hit the target!)

  (Note: I absolutely love the new disposable cleansing cloths on the market today. I wish they had been available all my homemaking days! They are relatively inexpensive, durable, and, best of all disposable. I think they are the most sanitary way to clean around the toilet. As long as my budget allows, I will never be without them.)

- Sweep and mop floor

  (Here also, I use the disposable cloths for mopping. I love the idea of not spreading germs but throwing them away instead.)

- Clean and dust all decorations and nick-nacks

Bedrooms

- Remove cobwebs

- Change sheets

- Dust

- Vacuum

All Other Rooms

- More of the same

If there is a room that is slightly different from all the others—the laundry room is one example—then look at it closely and see what specific things need to be done there. If it *is* the laundry room, then wipe off the top of the washer and dryer in addition to all the other things.

Can you think of more? Go ahead and add it to this list if you can. Remember, only attempt one room per day so that you don't become overwhelmed. These steps are easy and go quickly when done frequently. Some rooms may not need weekly attention. In such a case, rotate other non-weekly rooms into that time slot.

Fringe Benefits

Performing your 5x5x5's each day will eventually affect your Bonus Room step. Some days you will be ready to do your 5x5x5 step and realize that all the surface stuff is already done. At that point you will have the choice to either skip that room for that day or knock off one of the items from your *Bonus Room* chore list. If your kitchen is the bonus room for the day, you could scour the sink, clean the drip pans, clean out your microwave, or thoroughly wash the counter tops as part of your 5x5x5's. Then, when it comes time to do your *Bonus Room* step, that particular job will already be done. Yea!

Confessions

Sometimes I think I am a bit of a featherbrain. I guess I shouldn't confess such things. But, honestly! Some of the things that I think and do (and especially the things I *used* to think and do) make me shake this lightweight head of mine in disbelief. For example, in my pre-organized days, I very rarely cleaned the drip pans on my stove.

(Drip pans—You know what those are, don't you? They are those little trays that sit directly under each burner on the top of your range that are designed to catch any food that happens to spill, splatter, or boil over.)

Back then, the main color of drip pans that was readily available was silver. Black ones were just coming onto the market, but they were few and far between and quite expensive. Personally, I didn't know anyone who owned such extravagant drip pans. And certainly, only in my dreams did I ever think I would!

But then one day a brilliant idea struck me as I stood gazing at my despicable, thickly encrusted, half-black drip pans. I was just about to plunge head-long into my yearly obligation of cleaning them when I realized that I was on the verge of having the drip pans of my dreams—the *black* ones! If I didn't clean them now (an idea which sounded amazingly appealing), within a short period of time they would be *completely* black and everyone would think I had splurged and gotten the new sleek, beautiful, black ones! Whoa! Sometimes brilliance just strikes out of the blue.

Now, I am not typically a fast moving person, but the speed at which I put away the rubber gloves, scouring pads, and cleanser was nothing short of astonishing. As I left the kitchen that day, I felt a certain sense of satisfaction knowing that I had come up with a solution to one of life's most perplexing little problems. Women everywhere would benefit from importance of my discovery.

Then one day my dreams were dashed. During one of her visits to our home, my dear little old Aunt Sylvia (affectionately known to us as Auntie), spied my nearly perfect drip pans. Well, she was from the old school, apparently, because when I walked into the kitchen I found her standing at my kitchen sink furiously scrubbing those encrusted drip pans!

My heart sank! All those months of hard work…down the drain. "No! No! Auntie," I screeched. "I am *letting* them get black!" She stopped and looked at me for a moment, then promptly turned her attention back to the drip pans and proceeded to scrub with all her might.

I had to start all over.

Well, now, of course, I shake my head when I remember that whole line of reasoning. Did I really think someone would walk into my kitchen and actually think those drip pans were the lovely black ones? Oh, please! (My cheeks are burning as I confess this to you.)

But the burning has just begun, I'm afraid. There's more.

When I mentioned the cleaning of decorations and nick-nacks, I must confess that I never used to do that. I always cleaned the tops of flat surfaces, and that's it! It just never occurred to me that dust, grease, and grime could build up on other, non-flat, non-horizontal surfaces. Then one day (after learning that I should), I began to clean other surfaces in my home. Included in that category was a colorful, ceramic chicken that had been sitting on my kitchen windowsill for years. I gave the old gal a good hot bath in soapy water and when I pulled her out and dried her off, she was a whole different color than I thought. She was bright and beautiful. So, now I know. Greasy dirt, dust, and grime will adhere to almost any surface—up and down, curvy, round, slanted, whatever. So, we need to recognize that fact and clean all surfaces, not just the flat ones.

How Long Should It Take?

How long it takes you to do the five-step *Snappy Daily Routine* will depend on a number of factors. It will depend on how quickly you work, how far behind each room is when you first begin, and on what other obligations you have. For example, if you have small children at home, it will almost certainly take you longer than a mother whose children are in school.

In my pre-org days, if I had wanted to keep track of how long it took me each day to do my housework, I would have needed something more than a kitchen timer. I would have needed a calendar. But now, a simple kitchen timer will do the trick. Amazing, huh?

As a rule of thumb, you can figure on getting everything done in about an hour to an hour and a half. (Finishing the last of the laundry can take longer if there are multiple loads to do.)

I know that that may sound like a long period of time to you, but for me, thinking of getting everything done in an hour to an hour and a half was like being set free from a jail sentence. In my pre-organized days, I puttered around doing a little of this and a little of that, for hours on end. In fact, it never ended. It was like being caught in a revolving door, with no beginning and no end. The work was non-stop.

Now, the work that I do is fast, furious, and focused. It is performed at a heart-pounding, sweat-producing rate. But, the glorious part about it is—there is an end in sight. I like to compare it to going to the gym and putting in a good hour of intensive aerobic exercise. When you are done, you have accomplished more than you could in a whole day of dawdling around.

Your Power Hour

The five-step *Snappy Daily Routine* could be called your power hour! It is the hour of your day that you accomplish the bulk of your work.

> *Note: There is only one way you can get the bulk of your work done in such a short amount of time. And that is if you have established the habits and disciplines of responsibility in your life and if you have also trained each member of your family to take responsibility for themselves as well. This one simple factor will forever change your workload!*

> *When you don't have to spend huge chunks of time picking-up after people, then your work can be done in a fraction of the time. And not only that, but the work you do now can be the deeper stuff that you may not have had the energy or desire to tackle before, back when picking-up sapped you of your daily allotted energy. Consequently, the quality of your finished product will be much higher, the time you spent much less, and the freedom of life you gain much greater.*

Because of my power hour, I am free each day to pursue other interests in my life. And you can be too. It may be to start your own business, to spend more time with the precious young lives that have been entrusted into your care, to take up a hobby, to develop a skill, to give to your community, or anything else that is in your heart to do.

I am not saying that the power hour is easy. Goodness knows, it isn't. But it is so well worth the effort! You know how good you feel after exercising? Well, you will feel just as good after giving everything you've got each day to the *Snappy Daily Routine*—only better!

In Review

So, there you have it…the *Snappy Daily Routine* that will get your heart rate up, your house whipped into shape, and your self-confidence brimming. And guess what…it's only 5 simple steps.

#1. Do the breakfast dishes

#2. Plan tonight's dinner

#3. Start a load of laundry

#4. Do your 5x5x5's

#5. Bonus room

I was once a scatterbrained, undisciplined, unfocused, out-of-control, perfectionist. Whew! What a recipe for disaster! But this plan empowered me to stay focused and on task because it was so logical that it made sense to me and so simple that I could stick with it day after day.

If it is results you want, then this simple plan delivers.

CHAPTER 17

When You're Done, You're Done!

 $\mathcal{T}$ om and I have been blessed with two lovely children, a son and a daughter. They are all grown up now, but back when they were young and I had finally gotten my life in order, I began to have a dream.

Mary and I were teaching organization classes quire regularly and I began to dream of the day when my daughter, Lori, would grow up and join us in teaching these classes. Well, that day has come.

Actually, the picture is a little different than I had imagined. Mary's life branched in a whole different direction. She got a job outside her home that turned into a great career and so no longer has the time to devote to teaching classes. When she stepped down from teaching, Lori was a natural to step right into that position. So now, Lori and I teach as a team. She is so great at it that she amazes me. (OK, I know. I'm her mom and probably a little biased, but still, when I listen to her, I'm inspired, challenged, and energized. She truly *is* gifted!)

She brings to the table a whole different perspective and a level of wisdom that is simply over-the-top. She identifies with the younger generation who are now raising their own families, as she is hers. She is absolutely invaluable to this team.

One of the things that Lori has observed is that when she follows the steps outlined in this book, that her job as home manager is so much easier than when she just wings it:

A Word From Lori

The thing I appreciate the most about having a structured plan to follow is that "When you're done—you're done!" Once you've finished all the steps, you can quit for the day. That was so freeing to me. When I don't follow the plan, I tend to work all day long, because there is no quitting place. But on the plan, I know when I'm finished. And quitting at that point doesn't make me feel guilty, because I've accomplished all that I set out to do, and my house looks great. I can then do the things I want and love to do...WITHOUT GUILT!

Then, the next day, I begin again and work only, ONLY, until I've completed the necessary steps. I love what the Snappy Daily Routine does for my house AND for my life. Some days when my schedule is hectic and I get caught in the whirlwind of the life and I forget (or choose not) to follow the plan, I always regret it, especially about a week down the road. I always remind myself how wonderful life is ON the plan and bring myself back to it."

Thank you Lori, for that observation. The beauty of the plan is "When you're done—you're done!"

I love that lifestyle! Because I have better things to do with my life than to spend it cleaning my house! And yet, without a clean, I am hampered from accomplishing anything else.

The Snappy Daily Routine gives me the advantage I need to succeed in every other area of my life.

Yea, for structure and order; they set me free!

Lights Out!

*Y*awn! You've had a full, productive day, and now it's time to turn in for the night. The children are all tucked in, things are winding down and you're ready to hit the hay.

But before you do, you need to make a quick pass through the house looking for incidental disorder. Pick up and put away the occasional item that was accidentally left out and straighten any disorder (a rug that is askew, sofa pillows out of place, a throw that has gotten mussed, coasters on end tables, water rings on the kitchen counter, place mats crooked, etc.). It's called your "Lights Out" routine. It only takes a few seconds of your time, but yields tremendous rewards.

Crispness

"Crispness" will greet you the first thing in the morning! That's what you want to see when you first enter a room. It is like a breath of fresh air, sunlight streaming in through your window, a friend greeting you with a cheerful smile. Crispness gives you a lift the instant you see it. It sets the tone and mood for your whole day.

Small effort—great rewards!
Good night, sleep well, sweet dreams!

Graduation Day
Kudos to You, Soldier

*W*ell, you made it. You've come through Boot Camp with flying colors and you are graduating today. I am so proud of you. You amaze me! Just look how great you're doing.

You dedicated yourself to getting your life in order and you did it the right way, by starting the work on the inside of you. You've tackled your less than desirable habits and replaced them with some really great ones. Responsibility saturates every fiber of your being! You work it. You live it. You exude it. *Responsibility* is who you are. You've learned that it is the single most important element to your success. You are lost without it.

You know that your life is far too valuable to spend it "cleaning house" all day—every day, and yet, you love a clean house. You thrive on it. It brings joy to your heart and contentment to your soul. That is why it is absolutely vital that you make the most of your time by planning your work and working your plan. It is always better to work smarter than to work harder.

You know that you are cheating your family when you become a slave to them. You also know that there are no *rights* without *responsibilities* and you are determined to teach that truth to your children. You know that they will go far in life if you teach them this valuable truth and that they will suffer consequences all the days of their lives if they never learn it.

Can you see what great shape you are in? You rock! I believe in you...so much. It is my heart's desire to see you fulfill your every dream, reach your every goal, and become more than you ever thought possible. It is well within your ability.

Now you are ready to step into the next phase of organization with boldness and confidence because you know that the steps you take from here on out will not be sabotaged by the work of your own hands.

You are ready! You are ready to plunge into all the wondrous, dazzling STUFF you have acquired over the years. The things that you have shoved and stuffed into closets, cupboards, drawers. The things that loom larger than life everywhere you look. The things that seemingly have no rhyme or reason. All of your priceless possessions. All of the wonderful, delightful things that you hold dear, but at the same time, make you want to scream.

You are ready. You can do it. I know you can. All you need now is a simple plan to follow.

Of course, if you wanted to, you could even hire a professional organizer to come in and do the organizing for you.

What? You thought I didn't believe in hiring someone else to do the work for you?

Ah, I never said that. I said it would be a waste to hire someone to get your house organized IF you didn't possess the values, skills, and disciplines to keep it organized. Now that you do, hiring someone would be a viable option.

But you certainly don't have to hire anyone. Like I said, you are quite capable of doing it yourself. The choice is yours. But if you do choose to do it yourself, you will need a good plan to follow. A simple, logical, step-by-step guide to walk you through the process.

Just as there was a simple method for getting your house whipped into shape and keeping it that way, there is logical method for getting every single item in your house organized.

In my next book, "Clutter Busters: Organizing the Stuff", I will take you step by step through that process. You will learn to eliminate clutter and to establish a place for everything else. I will show you how to set up a super storage system that will knock your socks off. You will experience the thrill of living in a clutter-free zone because all the lesser-used items are stored away neatly in labeled, categorized containers. Yet, these items can be easily located and quickly retrieved when needed—even at a moment's notice! Who says you can't have your cake and eat it too?

Weedin' The Wardrobe

Does the old saying, "You can't see the forest for the trees" remind you of looking for something in your closet? Well, in "Organizing the Stuff" I will show you how to weed through your over crowded closet, keeping only *what's in, what fits,* and *what's in season.* And then I'll show you how to logically arrange what you keep in a way that will make it easy to find what you are looking for quickly and easily. With a nominal investment of money and time, your closet can look like a close cousin to one of those dreamy custom design closets in magazines we all drool over.

The Joy Of Cooking

Is your kitchen a joy to work in? It can be, if it is set up properly. If it is streamlined, organized, and arranged in a logical, workable order you will be able to do everything you need to do with fewer steps, in less time, and with less effort. And the clean-up will be a snap, too! If you love to cook but hate the hassle, then "Clutter Busters: Organizing the Stuff" will help you rediscover the joy of cooking by helping you get your kitchen deliciously organized.

Paper Trail

Paper, paper, paper! Oh, ugh! Too many papers, not enough time or space? Well, you can cut that paper mountain down to size and not sacrifice the good stuff in the process. A certain amount of paper is a necessity of life. What you do with it will help determine the quality of that life. If the stacks of paper exceed the space for living, you're in for a miserable existence. Not to mention the fact that once in a while it becomes necessary to actually *find* certain pieces of that paper. Sometimes, in a hurry. Well, there is a neat, concise, orderly way to store all the necessary papers so that they are readily accessible, easy to locate, and quick and easy to re-file for future reference.

Training Your Children

I once heard a wise old woman tell a story about how, if you give a man a fish, you will feed him for a day. But if you teach a man to fish you will feed him for a lifetime. Oh, I guess that wise old woman was me in the second chapter of this book. Well, guess what? What was true in chapter 2 is still true now. Knowledge. The world revolves around it and one of the main jobs of parenting is to impart knowledge to your children. You want them to be the very best they can be, to grow into responsible, competent, reliable, highly motivated adults. But that doesn't happen all by itself. You have to teach them, train them, spend time with them, and most of all, give them an excellent example to follow—you! Well "Clutter Busters: Organizing the Stuff" will help you do just that. We will explore ways to patiently, yet firmly, guide your children into the wonderful world of responsibility.

We will also help you get those little darlings to take on their fair share of responsibility around the house. SHARE THE LOAD! That's my motto. We all live in this house, why shouldn't we all take care of it?

And Much, Much, More!

We will explore all of these topics...AND MUCH, MUCH MORE in "Clutter Busters: Organizing the Stuff"!

And Now, Thank You

I want to take this opportunity to thank you for allowing me to be a part of your life. If I have been able to help you in some small way, I count it my great joy. I look forward to sharing more with you SOON.

May God bless you and keep you in all your ways.

Special Offer

Now, here is a special offer just for you…

You can contact us for a personal appearance to teach your mom's group, women's ministry, family support club, or other organization a four-hour seminar covering a cross section of both books.

For further information go on line at **www.theclutterbustersclub.com.**